Ministry for the Third Millennium

INNOVATIONS IN MINISTRY

Models for the Twenty-first Century

LYLE E. SCHALLER

ABINGDON PRESS / Nashville

Innovations in Ministry
Models for the Twenty-first Century

Copyright © 1994 by Abingdon Press

This book is printed on recycled, acid-free paper.

Library of Congress Cataloging-in-Publication Data

Schaller, Lyle E.
    Innovations in ministry : models for the twenty-first century /
Lyle E. Schaller.
        p.   cm.—(Ministry for the third millennium)
    Includes bibliographical references.
    ISBN 0-687-27105-3 (pbk. : alk. paper)
    1. Church management. 2. Protestant churches—United States.
3. Church growth—Protestant churches. I. Title. II. Series.
BV652.S33 1994
262'.0068—dc20   93-31950
                                                       CIP

\# 28709192

98 99 00 01 02 03 — 10 9 8 7 6 5 4

MANUFACTURED IN THE UNITED STATES OF AMERICA

To
J. Timothy Ahlen
Harvey Kneisel
Barbara Oden
Robert Tschannen-Moran

CONTENTS

INTRODUCTION

A persuasive argument can be made that the first three decades of the nineteenth century stand out as the most exciting era in the history of American Protestantism. The leaders of that day enjoyed the opportunity of pioneering an unprecedented variety of innovations. That era saw the Methodists and Baptists begin to emerge as the two largest Protestant religious bodies on the North American continent. The Plan of Union of 1801 between the Presbyterians and Congregationalists marked the beginning of a new form of interdenominational cooperation. An increasing proportion of the ministers came out of the working classes. The Second Great Awakening, revivalism, the invention of religious camp meetings, the Haystack Prayer meeting, and the challenge of foreign missions also mark that era. The first theological seminaries were born. A range of new nondenominational agencies was founded, such as the American Bible Society (1816), The American Sunday School Union (1824), the American

Peace Society (1828), and the American Tract Society (1825). The ecclesiastical climate was supportive of new ventures in ministry. Tradition, social status, and wealth no longer were as influential as they had been in the eighteenth century.

Perhaps the third most exciting era in American Protestantism was in the quarter century following the Civil War, when tens of thousands of new congregations, both black and white, were founded, the missionary movement reached its zenith, the Sunday school movement fostered a new era of interchurch cooperation, the central role of the laity was finally affirmed, the western frontier challenged the mavericks to try out new forms of ministry, and new denominations were born.

From this observer's perspective, the second most exciting era in the history of American Protestantism is the last quarter of the twentieth century. One reason for that assessment is the contemporary openness to new forms of ministry, the birth of a new expression of the faith through music, a more sophisticated use of television to communicate the gospel, and the emergence of new forms of interchurch cooperation based on the initiative of pastors and/or congregations.

While some may deplore the "consumerism" of this era, the generations born after 1955 are forcing the churches to be more sensitive to the religious needs of people. As the churches respond, new forms of ministry are being created. Another result is that new records in total church attendance in American Protestantism are being set year after year. To be more precise, the number of people worshiping in Protestant churches on the typical weekend in 1993 was larger than the total in 1953 or 1973 or 1983.

It is true that tens of thousands of small neighborhood churches, both urban and rural, are dying. The widespread ownership of the private automobile, that network of excellent paved streets and highways, the erosion of traditional institutional loyalties, the demand for choices, and the shift to a nongeographical base for meeting and making new friends are five of the threats that have undermined the small geographical parish. However, those are also five of the forces behind the emergence of thousands of large, vital, high quality, seven-day-a-week regional churches.[1]

Many will contend that the most influential factor behind the health, vigor, and vitality of contemporary American Protestantism is the recognition that the laity can be trusted to do ministry. That is a central theme of this book.

Another reason for the health and vitality of contemporary American Protestantism has been the growing capability of the churches to respond to the recent sharp increase in the diversity within American society. The middle third of the twentieth century was marked by a high degree of homogeneity in our culture. "One size fits all" was a slogan that worked reasonably and effectively. It was expressed in denominational hymnals, in the design of Sunday school materials, in the curriculum for seminary students, in the format for Sunday morning worship, in radio and later the three major television networks, in general-circulation denominational magazines, in the design of vacation Bible schools, in youth ministries, in strategies for evangelism and missions, and in the polity of the denomination.

Back in the 1930s, general-circulation magazines, such as *Life, Look,* and the *Saturday Evening Post,* prospered with this assumption that America was one large homogeneous audience.

Today the experts in marketing describe this country as a sea of diversity. That is reflected in the specialization of magazines, in the carving out of a distinctive niche by radio stations, and on the shelves of the supermarket. It also is reflected in the living arrangements of Americans, in their marital status, in the affirmation of their distinctive ethnic heritages, in the agendas of the dual-income households, in the concerns of the single-parent family, and in the way people dress. We have become a highly diverse culture.

The capability of many, but not all (!) Protestant congregations to respond creatively and effectively to this diversity is one reason why this can be identified as the second most exciting era in the history of American Protestantism. The introduction of drama and a new era in music have revolutionized worship. Television has transformed preaching. The expansion of the teaching ministry from Sunday school to a seven-day-a-week schedule has resulted in record numbers of adults engaged in continuing serious and in-depth Bible study. A new generation of teenagers has transformed youth ministries. The accumulation of unprecedented quantities of wealth in the pockets of self-identified "middle-class Americans" has sharply changed our approach to church finances. The continuing deterioration of large public school systems has created a new set of reasons for parents to enroll their children in Christian schools. The redefinition of the role of denominations, congregations, the clergy, and the laity have radically changed how we do outreach, missions, and evangelism.

This new series of books, *Ministry for the Third Millennium,* is designed to speak to leaders who (a) accept the fact that next year will not be a carbon copy of 1955; (b) are open to looking at new models for ministry and outreach; (c) agree the automobile is here to stay; (d) recognize that television has replaced religion as the single most influential force in shaping American culture, although it is not necessary to applaud that change; (e) believe that the worshiping community continues to be the number-one institutional expression of Christ's church; and (f) affirm that the needs and wants of people are at least as important as ecclesiastical traditions in formulating a strategy for ministry and outreach.

While a couple of overlapping areas of congregational life are discussed, the primary focus of this volume is on encouraging congregations to use off-campus ministries as part of a larger strategy for reaching new waves of immigrants to these shores and new generations of American-born residents.

The primary purpose of this book is to lift up several models of ministry that impress this observer as promising approaches for the beginning of the third millennium since the birth of Christ. The contemporary concern about full disclosure requires a statement about this observer's bias, or what I would describe as an earned opinion. After thirty-three years of working with congregations, pastors, volunteer leaders, specialized staff, and members from more than six dozen religious traditions plus scores of independent churches, I am convinced that congregational life in American Protestantism is healthier, stronger, and sounder than ever before in my lifetime. The vitality, relevance, and sensitivity of ministry in most of today's Protestant congregations is impressive!

Such a positive diagnosis cannot be offered about the state of every congregation. It also is true that American Catholicism is facing unprecedented problems. Likewise, several Protestant denominational systems are overdue for reform, and some will survive only if they are reformed.

That bias explains the reason behind the inclusion of the first chapter. The good news greatly exceeds the bad news about the current state of American Protestantism!

The second chapter elaborates on that same point. While it is true that several of the mainstream denominations have cut back sharply on launching new ministries, the vacuum created by those cutbacks is being filled by others. God lifts up the initiating leaders required for a continuing expansion of Christ's church.

The third chapter introduces a theme that is central to one of the challenges to today's churches. This is the value of clearly, precisely, and accurately identifying that segment of the total population that a specific ministry is designed to reach. This theme deserves a separate chapter because it is central to every model of ministry described here.

Few readers will argue that preachers should continue to use horses for their transportation today. A new era has brought new tools for carrying the gospel to people. One is the automobile. A second is television. One of the most effective means of undermining the ministry of any Christian organization is to seek to perpetuate yesterday. The fourth chapter describes a half dozen changes that truly are paradigm shifts. Anyone seeking to implement many of the new models described here must understand the radical nature of these changes.

The fifth chapter is not only the longest section of this book, it is the heart of it. This introduces a field-tested and proven model of multiplying ministries that may be the most promising model in today's marketplace of ecclesiastical ideas. It calls for a new partnership that redefines the role of denominations, raises the expectations projected of the laity, and calls for a reappraisal of congregational priorities. When JV Thomas challenged me to look into the Key Church Strategy in Texas, he aroused my curiosity. One result was that I met dozens of committed, creative, and effective pioneers in new expressions of ministry. Most important, I discovered that the Key Church Strategy works. Another result is this book.

Practical implementations of the Key Church Strategy are described in the sixth and seventh chapters.

Overlapping that strategy is the recognition by an increasing number of congregations that their call to faithfulness requires more than one meeting place. That option is described in the eighth chapter.

For some readers, the only controversial issue in this book is the use of the Christian day school as the heart of two different models. We are now in what some identify as the fourth era or generation of Christian day schools in the United States. Most of the objections to the immigrant schools and to the segregationist academies of yesteryear do not apply to the contemporary models that are described in the ninth chapter.

My pragmatic nature and my Depression ethic cause me to be sympathetic to the cries of those who worry about paying the bills. Here again we see new models for the twenty-first century, and a few of those are discussed in the last chapter.

Finally, I am indebted to a greater degree to a larger number of people than for any previous book. I am grateful for their comments, cooperation, courtesy, ideas, insights, openness, patience, questions, reflections, suggestions, and wisdom. An incomplete list includes Tim Ahlen, Bob Bull, Steve Conger, Stan Copeland, Karen Curtis, Richard Dunagin, Lanny Elmore, Dick Flynn, Joe Hall, Les Hoffmann, C. B. King, Harvey Kneisel, Rick Linamen, J. Mark Martin, Barbara Oden, Mike Piazza, Don Poest, Randy Pope, Mike Rasmussen, Ray Schwartz, Michael Scrogin, Lon Snyder, Bob Tschannen-Moran, JV Thomas, Benny Vaughan, Rick Warren, Woodie Webb, and Craig Wilson. Naming them does not carry with it the implication that they should share the blame for any misstatements of fact, stupid interpretations, or ridiculous conclusions that may be found in this book. All it means is that I am indebted to them, and I am grateful.

This book is dedicated to four individuals who are pioneering new eras in ministry for the third millennium of Christ's church.

1.

BAD NEWS IS BETTER NEWS THAN GOOD NEWS

Two of the most significant life-and-death trends of the twentieth century in the United States illustrate the title of this opening chapter. Each can be introduced in autobiographical terms.

In April 1923 scarlet fever was still a common disease. A four-and-one-half-year-old boy named John caught it and became very ill. His pregnant mother tended him around the clock. He recovered, but his mother contracted this highly contagious disease from her only child. Several days later, on April 19, the high fever induced labor pains, and it became apparent a premature birth would soon be the result. The frantic father telephoned the local midwife, who lived two miles away, to hurry over, and he also telephoned the family doctor. A late snowstorm had turned the unpaved country road into a quagmire of mud. Two miles from his office, the physician telephoned to report his car was stuck in the mud. The father hitched his team of horses to a wagon and drove through the mud to pick up the doctor and bring him to what appeared to be his dying wife.

Within the space of fifteen minutes, according to the oral tradition, three people arrived in that second-floor bedroom on the southwestern corner of this ten-year-old farmhouse. The first was the anxious midwife, who arrived on very short notice. The second was a tiny, red, wizened, baby who was six weeks early. Third was the physician, who was a few minutes late. The doctor quickly appraised the situation, cut the umbilical cord, and discarded the infant on a pile of quilts in the corner. "That baby doesn't have a chance of surviving," he declared, "and I'll need all of your help if we hope to save the life of the mother."

"This baby is going to live!" retorted the midwife as she gently reclaimed the baby boy from where the physician had placed him. She cleaned him up and wrapped him in a soft cotton blanket. "It'll be a miracle if either one is alive tomorrow," argued the physician, but the determined midwife persisted. The miracle occurred. The mother survived for another forty-one years, and the premature baby is the author of this book.

That physician, however, was right. For that day, it was a miracle. In 1923, for every one million live births in the United States, 6,650 mothers died in childbirth—a remarkable drop from only three years earlier, when 7,990 mothers died in childbirth for every one million births.

In 1949, when that premature baby became a father for the first time, only 900 mothers failed to survive the birth of a baby out of every one million births. In 1990, when that premature baby became the grandfather of twins, the maternal death rate had dropped to 75 for every million live births in the United States.

In only seven decades, from 1920 to 1990, the maternal death rate in the United States had plunged 99 percent! Most of today's news stories, however, focus on one of two story lines. One points out that the maternal death rate for black mothers in America in 1990 was 184 per one million births, more than three times the rate of 56 per million births for white mothers. The second story line is that the maternal death rate in the United

States is not as low as it is in four or five European countries. Bad news is better news than good news.

One of the major news stories of 1937, the year that premature baby turned fourteen, was about the unprecedented number of people killed on the nation's roads. The total reached 39,643 in 1937. That not only was a new record, but the number of traffic deaths per 100,000 population reached 30.8, a ratio never reached before or since. An equally useful indicator is that 1937 record number of traffic deaths averaged 14.7 per 100 million vehicle miles driven.

What did that record number of traffic deaths portend for the future? By 1992 the number of motor vehicle miles traveled on American highways was nearly nine times the 1937 total. A straight line projection of the 1937 death rate on American highways would have meant that in 1992 approximately 350,000 people would be killed in motor vehicle accidents. The number of highway deaths in 1992 was slightly under 39,000, well below that 1937 total, and down from the record of 54,600 in 1972. For comparison purposes, in 1991 approximately 60,000 Americans died from unnecessary surgical procedures. It is safe to drive to the operating room, but don't go in!

In 1937, one out of every 3,290 Americans was killed in a highway accident. In 1992 it was one in 6,500 residents, despite that ninefold increase in motor vehicle miles traveled.

That improvement in the highway safety record meant that at the end of 1992, well over three million Americans were still alive who would have been dead if the death rates on the highway for the years 1983–1992 had been the same as for 1937. The bad news, of course, is that these three million survivors will be adding to the financial burden on the Social Security trust fund.

The moral of this account about improvements in highway safety is simple. The traffic accident that kills seven people on a holiday weekend is front page news. The annual report from the National Highway Traffic Safety Administration that tells of new record lows in the ratio of deaths to motor vehicle miles traveled is hidden on page 9, if it even makes the paper. Bad news is better news than good news.

Many years ago I stopped in to visit with a newspaper reporter friend who covered the City Hall beat. On the wall above his desk was a sign that read "Bad News Is Better News Than Good News." That slogan reflects what motivates people to purchase newspapers; it guides the selection of stories for the evening television news report and the choice of stories for the hour-long "news magazines" on television. That slogan also reflects the coverage by the media of organized religion in the United States.

The Bad News Is There!

There is an abundance of bad news! From the perspective of the year 2018, perhaps the most far reaching bad news is the inability of today's theological seminaries to attract adequate numbers of highly competent, exceptionally gifted, deeply committed, and clearly extroverted adults born after 1965 who possess a compelling call to the parish ministry. It may be unrealistic to expect seminaries to recruit people for the parish ministry. The time may have arrived for a new system for enlisting, training, screening, and credentialing the next generation of parish pastors.[1]

One possible scenario for 2018 is that most of the 225,000 Protestant congregations now averaging under 120 at worship that survive for another three decades will be served by bivocational ministers and bivocational teams, most of the 85,000 congregations averaging 120 to 325 at worship will be served by seminary-trained ministers, and many of those averaging over 325 at worship will be served by staffs trained in large teaching churches. (In 1993 approximately one-third of all Protestant churchgoers on a typical weekend worshiped in congregations that average less than 120 at worship, one-third in congregations averaging 120 to 325, and one-third in that 7 percent of all American Protestant congregations averaging over 325 at worship.)

This surfeit of bad news includes the scandals associated with a couple of television evangelists, the sharp decline in membership in a dozen Protestant denominations, the closing of eight Protestant churches on the average day, the hundreds of pastors who are fired every year, the decisions of the United States Supreme Court that have undermined the free exercise clause of the First Amendment, the number of male preachers who have not been able to keep the zipper closed on their trousers, the trend that finds two-thirds of the congregations in several denominations either on a plateau in size or declining in numbers, the staff cutbacks in the national offices of several denominations and in the National Council of Churches, the decision by Harvard and other universities founded by Christian churches to object to the policy of many private Christian secondary schools that limit their faculty and trustees to professing Christians, the decision by a federal bankruptcy court judge that a church had to refund the tithes given to that church by a couple who subsequently declared bankruptcy, the number of colleges and universities founded by the churches that have severed their ties to that religious body, the sexual abuse of women and children by hundreds of male clergy, the litigation that has split congregations, the decision by hundreds of thousands of Germans since 1990 to renounce their church membership in order to escape the church tax collected by the German government and passed on to the churches, the schisms within American denominational families, the decision every year by several thousand disillusioned pastors either to opt for early retirement or to leave the professional ministry completely, the shrinking number of young white males enrolling in mainline Protestant denominational seminaries and in Roman Catholic seminaries, the opposition by the neighbors to plans by a congregation to expand its facilities, the closing of dozens of religious magazines, the embezzlement of funds by a trusted church treasurer, the sharp decline in Sunday school attendance since the peak years of the 1960s, the cutback in new church development by several denominations, and the closing of hundreds of Catholic and Lutheran parochial schools.

While far from a comprehensive list, that long paragraph illustrates the point that there is sufficient bad news to satisfy those who are seeking it.

The Good News Side

There also is sufficient bad news to conceal much of the good news, but the good news is there. Too often, however, it is well hidden. What is the good news? That is one theme of this book, but two dozen examples will illustrate the point that it is bountiful.

1. Between 1975 and 1992, the population of the United States increased by 18 percent, but the average worship attendance in white Protestant congregations rose by 22 percent. (We do not have comparable data for worship attendance in African American or Hispanic Protestant churches.)

2. Protestantism in the nation's three hundred central cities is alive, well, and probably healthier than ever before.[2] Scores of "Old First Church Downtown" congregations are carrying out exceptionally effective ministries. For some reason, a disproportionately large number carry the name "First Presbyterian Church" (or Westminster or Fourth or ?).

3. Back in the late 1960s and early 1970s, many church leaders wondered whether the young adults of that era, who displayed strong anti-institution attitudes and were dropping out of church by the millions, would ever come back. While most did not return to the congregation in which their parents were members, and many switched denominations, they are in church in huge numbers in the 1990s.[3]

A disproportionately large number of the post-1942 generations can be found in (a) new congregations and/or (b) large churches and/or (c) congregations that focus on the personal and religious needs of people rather than on the institutional or financial agenda of the church or denomination and/or (d) downtown churches in large cities and/or (e) nondenominational or independent congregations and/or (f) churches that place at the top of the list of their priorities preaching, teaching, and fast-paced worship and/or (g) churches that welcome the seekers, searchers, pilgrims, and others on a self-identified religious quest. The good news is that the number of congregations that meet four or five or six of those qualifications is increasing.

4. This newest religious revival, which also includes the active participation of millions born in the 1955–68 era, has been accompanied and nurtured by an exciting wave of creative new Christian music and drama.

Those who evaluate contemporary Christian music as bad news can be comforted by the fact that there still is a place and a demand for the traditional church that takes its mission seriously. That includes carefully planned and well organized traditional worship services, excellent preaching, high quality music, and a teaching ministry that reaches all generations. All of this must be grounded in a strong and abiding commitment to build an inclusive and diverse Christian community and to care for the community in which it is located. These traditional churches can and do attract and hold strong, talented, and dedicated lay leaders who share that commitment to Christ's ministry. An excellent example of a contemporary traditional congregation is the First Baptist Church of Worcester, Massachusetts.

5. One of the least publicized changes of the past several decades has been the greater emphasis given to grace, love, and hope and the reduced emphasis on guilt and fear in American Christianity. This change is most clearly visible in (a) the preaching in theologically conservative churches, (b) hymns written in the twentieth century, (c) the teaching ministries of the churches, and (d) inspirational Christian literature published since the 1970s. One example of this pronounced emphasis on grace and love is the number of hymns in the recently published hymnals that reflect the explanation of the atonement in terms of Christ's moral influence over believers, rather than by the classical theory

that Christ's death and resurrection represented a victory over sin and death, or that Christ's sacrificial death satisfied God's wrath against human sin (the restitution theory).

Whether this change represents good news or bad news will be determined by the theological position and value system of the reader, but it is a significant theme in contemporary Christian music.

6. While some feared that the demise of the neighborhood church marked the end of effective evangelistic outreach efforts, the successor, the regional church, has a far better evangelistic record. (See chapter 4.)

7. The American marketplace has produced an unprecedented demand by consumers for higher quality. That demand includes automobiles, food, electronic devices, medical care, motel rooms, retail facilities, preaching, the teaching ministries, pastoral care, and internal communication. A remarkable number of Protestant churches in America have been able to upgrade the quality of their ministry to meet that demand.

This has been accompanied in several denominations by systematic efforts to introduce the teachings of W. Edwards Deming and the concept of Total Quality Management into ecclesiastical organizations. One such effort, introduced by Ezra Earl Jones, has been to adapt this philosophy of leadership into annual conferences in The United Methodist Church under the label The Quest for Quality.

8. While it is still true that denominational meetings frequently focus their deliberations on the law, more and more congregations are building their ministry around God's gift of grace.

9. While much remains to be done, a broad slice of European-based white Protestantism in the United States has been able to respond to the religious needs of immigrants from the Pacific Rim.

10. The replacement of denominations and denominational offices as the principal players in interdenominational and interfaith cooperative ventures by pastors, congregations, and volun-

teer leaders has led to an unprecedented level of interchurch cooperation on the local scene. One of hundreds of examples of this is the ecumenical Community Help Center of Mt. Juliet, Tennessee, which is operated by a board of directors made up of representatives from twelve local churches (Church of the Nazarene, United Methodist, Southern Baptist, Catholic, Presbyterian, and nondenominational). This Help Center is a 501(c)3 corporation that provides emergency financial assistance and food and clothing to needy families. It is a central agency to which the local churches refer people who may ask for help from a church.

11. Even those denominations that have experienced substantial numerical losses in membership and churches have been able to point to areas of significant growth. For example, between 1974 and 1990 The United Methodist Church reported a net decrease of 1,900 congregations, and the number of small churches averaging fewer than 35 at worship grew from 9,600 to 10,800, but the number of large churches averaging 500 or more at worship increased by 23 percent from 449 to 552.

At the other end of the size scale, one of the most promising programs in United Methodism has been launched by the two annual conferences in Indiana. It is designed to enlist, train, place, and support licensed lay ministers to serve as bivocational ministers in smaller congregations. The program displays such promise that in late 1992 it received a major grant from the Lilly Endowment.

A program such as this could be designed by any denomination with a substantial number of small congregations. It could be enriched by the insights from Deming and total quality management. It also could be integrated into a larger strategy to heal the wounded birds that is described in chapter 7 as a part of a larger strategy to challenge the congregations with a surplus of discretionary resources.

12. Perhaps the most significant piece of good news is the renewed interest in the power of intercessory prayer. Several

congregations now have either a full-time or part-time minister of prayer on the staff. The breadth of that list is illustrated by the fact that it includes a Lutheran parish in Arizona, a United Church of Christ congregation in northeastern Ohio, and a Southern Baptist church in suburban Atlanta.

13. A long-time criticism of American Protestantism was that eleven o'clock Sunday morning was the most segregated hour of the week. Today thousands of Protestant congregations are truly multicultural and multiracial fellowships that include people from a huge range of social, economic, ethnic, racial, and educational backgrounds. Hundreds of charismatic churches probably are the most highly visible example of this, but that list also includes scores of small inner-city congregations plus those organized around a Christian day school that responds to the members' upwardly mobile ambitions for their children and those churches that focus on the transformational power of the gospel.

14. Back in the 1960s, the advice given to congregational leaders was "Find your missional outreach in your own backyard and do it." This advice has been taken literally by tens of thousands of congregational leaders and is being acted out all across the nation. Instead of sending their money away to hire someone to do "missions," these churches are spending larger sums in off-campus ministries in their own communities. Chapters 5, 6, 7, 8, and 9 offer examples of this piece of good news.

15. Several denominations have reported that registrations for their summer national youth convocation exceeded the capacity of the facilities, and a second convocation had to be scheduled to handle the overflow.

16. The Metro Synod of the Evangelical Lutheran Church in America has created a new focal point for ministry: "Health and Healing for Community and Church." Bishop Sherman G. Hicks has declared that this means the Synod "will be in partnership with congregations to transform our congregations into places where the healing ministry of Jesus and the gospel is central to

all that happens in the congregations, among the members, and in outreach to the community." This is one more example of the emerging relationship between regional judicatories and congregations as partners and is in contrast to the regulatory agency role of many regional judicatories.

An earlier emphasis on encouraging congregations to reclaim their responsibility for the total health of individuals, families, and institutions was pioneered by Midwestern Lutherans and Dr. Granger Westberg. This is the Parish Nurse Program. By 1993 more than a thousand parish nurses or ministers of health, some paid, some volunteer, were serving congregations across the United States. One goal is to make health awareness an integral part of a congregation's mission.[4]

17. The rhetoric about collegiality in ministry usually has exceeded the performance, but one place where this expression of staff relationships has been acted out for thirteen years is in the Anglican Diocese of Toronto in Canada. This "College of Bishops" operates around a consensus approach to decision making.

What makes this an especially notable experiment is that four of the five original members of the College, including Bishop Lewis Garnsworthy, the originator of the concept, have retired and been replaced, and that collegial style of ministry continues to flourish.

18. One of the most hopeful signs for the future is the emergence of several new parachurch organizations that have been clearly and precisely defined to undergird and strengthen the ministries of worshiping communities. This is in contrast to most of the earlier parachurch organizations that were organized to respond to unmet needs by doing ministry unilaterally. Two outstanding examples of this new expression of the parachurch movement are the Stephen Ministries in St. Louis, Missouri, and the Leadership Network in Tyler, Texas.

19. For many years both religious radio broadcasting and religious television programs were dominated by preachers and

evangelists who were not serving as pastors of worshiping communities. Today most of the preachers on religious television programs are parish pastors.

20. One of the best bits of good news is the active participation of a growing number of young white males and young black males in church on Sunday morning. For years, the pessimists were predicting that the churches were narrowing their constituency to women and old men. That is NOT the way the twentieth century will end!

21. One of the most significant pieces of good news has been the changes in scheduling Christian education. Once confined to an hour on Sunday morning, the teaching ministry is now spread throughout the week. One result is that in the early 1990s more adults were engaged, on a weekly basis, in the serious and continuing study of the Scriptures than ever before in American history.

22. For generations the organizational self-image of a Protestant congregation in the United States was a gathered community with its own private meeting place and served by a pastor and perhaps other paid staff as well as volunteer leaders. Its ministry was pointed to with pride as an in-house affair. In corporate terms, the Sunday school, the youth group, the choir, the benevolence committee, and every other activity or group were wholly owned subsidiaries. The congregation owned its ministry, controlled its ministry, possessed its ministry, and knew who to blame when something went wrong.

A new model has emerged that moves the congregation and its ministries away from the controlling center and toward the collaborating perimeter. The model is less protectionist and more dangerous, as control slips further and further away from the traditions that are associated with the church's name. Variations of this new model are described in chapters 5, 6, and 7.

An outstanding example of this new model is the Good News Community Church in Chicago. The Good News Community Church, affiliated with the United Church of Christ, is located on the far north side of Chicago, in what many consider a depressed inner-city neighborhood. It has been gathering for fifteen years a multiracial, multicultural, bilingual community of faith. With the traditional model, the Church might have little more to show for its work than the 100-plus people who now gather for worship on Sunday morning. Instead, having acted as the catalyst for rather than the controller of ministry, the Good News Community Church participates in a larger network of ministries—each a separately incorporated 501(c)3 organization—that has grown into a $2.5 million-per-year operation.

The larger network is known as Good News North of Howard, itself incorporated in May of 1978. This network, which coordinates the work of and provides specific benefits (e.g., a group insurance plan) to its member organizations, includes four other 501(c)3 organizations. The Good News Community Church is one of these four, being an equal partner with the others rather than an overarching umbrella. The other three are the Good News Educational Workshop, Peoples Housing, and Good News Partners.

The Good News Community Church worships in two services on Sunday morning, English and Spanish, except for the first Sunday of the month, when it worships in one bilingual communion service. Its pastoral staff of three—African American, European American, and Hispanic American—reflects the multiracial, multicultural, and bilingual nature of the church. In addition to many wholly owned traditional ministries (Gospel Choir, vacation Bible school, revivals, and Bible studies) the Good News Church operates a soup kitchen that feeds 110 hungry people a free evening meal seven nights a week. The soup kitchen is legally but not exclusively the ministry of the church, but it is largely controlled by the people who volunteer and work in it. This includes representatives from almost thirty congregations (Protestant, Catholic, Jewish) and organizations (service clubs, schools, etc.). They meet once a quarter and do what needs to be done to raise the necessary funds and establish the necessary policies and procedures. What the Good News Church loses in control, it gains in resources to serve more than 40,000 meals annually.

Another component of this larger ministry is the Good News Educational Workshop. To help pay the bills, many churches, especially urban churches, frequently rent out portions of their space (to day care centers and community organizations, etc.). In the case of Good News, however, there is more than just a landlord-tenant relationship. Although separate corporations, the church and the Educational Workshop share space, produce a joint newsletter, pay for umbrella insurance policies, and participate in each other's programs. The Educational Workshop is an alternative Christian day school, grades K-8, for sixty primarily low and moderate income students as well as an after-school reading tutorial program for forty second and third grade students from the local public school.

Two other components are Peoples Housing and Good News Partners. These corporations do not share space with the Church and the Educational Workshop. Peoples Housing concentrates on the rehabilitation of housing for low and moderate income people, especially families. It has rehabilitated more than 300 units of rental housing over the past decade, managing and maintaining them after construction has been completed. Peoples Housing has made extensive use of private and public funds to accomplish its mission. Good News Partners, on the other hand (like Habitat for Humanity), has shied away from government funding. It is a Christian response to the problems of poverty, aiming to help homeless people become homeowners. Good News Partners runs a shelter, a single-room occupancy hotel, and three cooperatively owned apartment buildings.

Each of these separate corporations has its own governing board, budget, sources of funding, program, policies, priorities, executive director, and paid staff. Each of these separate corporations chooses, however, to remain connected to one another through the Good News North of Howard umbrella. This facilitates long-range planning, coordinated fund raising, and pooling of staff or resources as need and opportunity arises.

Among the many advantages of this model are these: (1) it gives many more people many more ways to be involved than simply joining the church (as volunteers, board members, staff, financial contributors, and technical assistance providers for a particular ministry or area of interest); (2) it opens the doors to many sources of funding not traditionally available to a worshiping community; (3) it facilitates cooperation and coordination among separate but overlapping ministries; (4) it eliminates diversionary discussion over such objections as "But I don't believe that it is an appropriate area for us to be involved in when we have so many other high priorities here in our church"; (5) it minimizes the possibility that all the ministries will become overly dependent upon any one individual leader; (6) it can respond to a variety of needs of the people to be served; (7) it reduces inter-agency conflict because all are part of one network; (8) it makes efficient use of paid staff; and (9) it offers possibilities for cooperative arrangements with organizations that would not otherwise enter into a partnership with a Christian church.

Among the drawbacks to this model are these three: (1) it leaves people with the uneasy feeling that things are going on that they are associated with, but over which they do not have full and direct control; (2) the social ministries can easily eclipse the church community in both size and weight unless the network makes a conscious effort to the contrary; and (3) it requires a long tenured and highly committed, creative, and entrepreneurial personality, with above average skills in interpersonal relationships, to develop and maintain such a network.

23. A strong argument could be made that the best news at the end of the twentieth century is that when they are challenged, the laity do respond! This is a central theme of chapters 4, 5, 6, and 8 as well as the Good News North of Howard model described in the preceding paragraphs.

While the cause-and-effect relationship has yet to be proved, the rise of denominationalism in the first five or six decades of the twentieth century coincided with a growing dependency on the clergy. The extreme form of this was when the pastor could not be present on Sunday morning, the decision was made to cancel the scheduled gathering for the corporate worship of God. During the 1940–80 era, tens of thousands of people were hired to do what formerly had been done by volunteers in congregations. One result of the expanded role of the clergy in both congregational and denominational affairs was the decision by many creative and skilled laypersons to allocate their time and energy as volunteers to some other voluntary association. A second was the emergence of thousands of new independent congregations. A third was the inability of the clergy-dominated religious traditions to retain their "market share" of the generations of churchgoers born after 1942. A fourth was the decision by many of the lay program staff members to go to seminary as they saw the power that went with ordination. "If you can't beat 'em, join 'em."

The new pattern, however, is to share more responsibilities with lay volunteers.

24. Finally, while the churches were latecomers to this game, one of the most significant items of good news is the growing number of congregations that have expanded their teaching ministry to include a broad range of mutual support groups.

For several decades, the reluctance of the churches to move into this area of ministry meant the needs were being filled by secular organizations. These included mutual support groups for alcoholics, families with an alcoholic parent, persons going through a traumatic divorce, parents who had experienced the death of a child, adults still affected by the divorce of their parents a dozen years earlier, long-tenured employees who suddenly became unemployed, parents of a son who was dying of an AIDS-related illness, victims of child abuse, people recovering from drug addiction, parents about to adopt a child, and dozens of similar recovery or support groups. The entrance of the churches into this area of ministry has silenced many of the critics who were pointing out the growing irrelevance of the churches.

The creation of these mutual support groups that combine the learnings from the helping professions with the teachings of the Christian faith may be the fastest growing new model of ministry in the last third of the twentieth century.

But Not Everything Works!

While the purpose of this chapter is to point out that the bad news is overshadowed by the good news, it must be noted that occasionally new models do not work out as well as was anticipated.

One example is the famous Plan of Union of 1801 by which the Congregationalists and the Presbyterians agreed to work cooperatively in organizing new congregations on the Western frontier with a noncompeting missionary program. The Presbyterians did stay out of New England, but many of the new Congregational churches on the Western frontier eventually chose to unite with a local Presbytery. The Plan of Union really limited the growth of both denominations.

The last part of the nineteenth century and the first several decades of the twentieth saw the emergence of a broad effort at cooperation in new church development. This new expression of "comity" was intended to reduce competition, prevent the "overchurching" of communities, and enhance efficiency.

One result was that the higher the level of cooperation among the representatives of the various cooperating denominations, the smaller the number of new missions launched by these denominations and the larger the number of attractive church sites that were left to be available to noncooperating denominations.[5]

When the world's first fully enclosed shopping mall opened in the Minneapolis suburb of Edina in 1956, some hailed it as the new version of Main Street. During the next two decades retail trade did move from downtown to the mall. This trend raised a provocative question: Why not move the church from Main Street to the mall? One proponent of this change forecast that most of the conventional expressions of the church would disappear, and the church in the shopping mall would be the dominant institutional expression of the faith in the twenty-first century.

The United Church of Christ launched the Agora (marketplace) ministry in the Oakbrook shopping center in suburban Chicago. It opened in late 1964 and closed five years later. The most extravagant shopping mall church was the Marketplace Ministries in the Landmark center in Alexandria, Virginia. This four-level venture included a theater, a child-care center, a library, and other services, but was abandoned for lack of funds after four years by the Presbyterians and Methodists, who had provided the original finances. Another denomination picked it up, but they dropped it after two years. Today it is difficult to find anyone who even recalls the existence of that very expensive pioneering venture.

Dozens of other ministries opened in shopping malls and shopping centers. Some were new missions using this as a temporary meeting place. Others were counseling centers financed by the joint sponsorship of several congregations. A few continue as the primary or only meeting place for worshiping communities. By and large, however, the dream of the church in the shopping mall never fulfilled the dreams of the 1960s. One reason, of course, is the growing proportion of retail trade that has moved out of the malls into the giant superstores. The shopping malls also did not fulfill the dreams many retailers had when they rented space there nor did they achieve the hopes of many investors who lost money on these ventures.

Another dream that promised more than it delivered was the hope of replacing denominationally affiliated congregations with "ecumenical churches" that would serve people from several different religious traditions. That dream included the provision that these ecumenical churches would maintain an institutional affiliation with each of the four or five or six cooperating denominations. This dream has almost been fulfilled by scores of very large congregations that annually welcome newcomers from twenty or thirty or forty different Protestant and Catholic heritages. The big difference is that these congregations are affiliated with zero denominations, not four or five or six.

The grand design for that elimination of denominational rivalries was officially born in 1962 when four denominations came together to create the Consultation on Church Union. Over the years the participants grew to include representatives from nine denominations. The goal changed from one huge denominational merger to encouraging congregations to cooperate in ministry.

Finally, since 1960 several denominations have been persuaded to plant a new mission in a community that appeared to need another new church. Scores of these have grown into what today are called megachurches. Hundreds more are vigorous, healthy, vital, relevant, self-governing, self-propagating, self-financing, and self-expressing congregations. That is the good news. The bad news is that dozens of these new missions struggled with small numbers, low morale, mounting financial subsidies, and few newcomers until the time came when all concerned were ready for ecclesiastical euthanasia.

Not everything works, but that does not mean new models of ministry should not be tried. That is one bit of advice to keep in mind while reading the rest of this book. The second is that when the established religious systems do not respond to new needs, God will send someone else to fill that vacuum. That also is good news.

2.

FILLING IN THE VACUUM

During the first half of the twentieth century, Sears, Roebuck and Company, Montgomery Ward, and J. C. Penney competed to be the number one retailer to middle America. By 1960 it was clear that Sears had won that three-way race.

The last third of the twentieth century, however, brought several new competitors to the retailing scene. By 1993 two of these new competitors had moved to the head of the pack, and Sears trailed both Wal-Mart and KMart in retail sales.

As recently as 1973, well over 90 percent of all television sets were tuned in to one of the three major networks. Two decades later ABC, CBS, and NBC were dividing less than 63 percent of the market. Cable had brought scores of new competitors in to fill the gap created by the declining market share of the three big networks.

In 1963, imports accounted for 5.1 percent of all passenger cars sold in the United States. Thirty years later that proportion was up to 26 percent.

In 1949, AM radio stations attracted well over 90 percent of this nation's radio audience. By 1992 that proportion had plummeted to 15 percent, and more than 300 AM radio stations either closed shop in 1991 and 1992 or converted to FM. What filled the gap? The answer, of course, was FM radio and the compact disc (CD) player. For decades, aspirin was the common response to a headache. "Take two aspirin and go to bed" was a widely followed prescription for a cold or a headache. In 1985, however, it became legal to sell ibuprofen as an over-the-counter drug without a prescription. By 1993 it had won nearly one-half of the $2.7 billion annual market in the United States for pain relievers. Subsequently Naprosyn began to gain popularity and became a competitor for Advil, Motrin IB, Tylenol, aspirin, and other pain relievers.

A series of parallel tales can be told about what happened to magazine publishers, grocery stores, and other organizations designed to service the general public. Many organizations had difficulty in retaining the loyalty of old customers and even greater problems in winning the loyalty of new generations. Every institution that is designed to serve people must either win the allegiance of new generations or watch the clientele shrink in size. This is illustrated by newspapers, by AM radio stations, by national retail chains, by over-the-counter drugs, by automobile manufacturers—and by religious congregations.

This last example can be illustrated by looking at three Protestant denominations. In 1950 the Lutheran Church-Missouri Synod claimed 1.7 million baptized members in North America. During the next four decades, that total rose to 2.7 million. What was required to produce that net increase of a million in the baptized membership of this denomination? Among other factors the pastors reported they baptized more than 2.8 million children to produce that net gain of one million baptized members. (These calculations exclude the number of adults who were baptized during those four decades.)

In 1968 the Evangelical United Brethren Church merged with the Methodist Church to create a new denomination of 11.1 million confirmed members. During the next twenty-five years

(1969–1993 inclusive) a total of nearly three million confirmed members of this new denomination had their names removed from the membership rolls because of death. (An uncounted number had moved away and/or dropped into inactivity or died, and subsequently their names were removed from congregational rosters by action of a charge conference.) Most of those members who died were not replaced, and that is the biggest single reason why the membership of this new denomination dropped by nearly 2.5 million during that quarter century. If the membership curve of this new denomination had paralleled the population growth of the United States, United Methodist membership at the end of 1993 would have been 14.3 million rather than 8.7 million. (It is worth noting that if the death rate of 1968 for adult Americans, age 40 and over, had been frozen at the 1968 level, instead of gradually declining year after year, that total would have been 3.3 million deaths rather than 3 million.)

A third pattern is illustrated by a 1993 report from the Home Mission Board of the Southern Baptist Convention. The researchers found this denomination had launched an average of 430 new churches annually during the previous nineteen years. Concurrently an average of 233 congregations were removed each year from Southern Baptist rolls. This meant that an average of 2.2 new congregations had to be planted to achieve a net gain of one.

For American Protestantism in general, if the goal is to remain on a plateau in size, it is necessary for a denomination to plant one new congregation annually for every 100 to 150 existing churches. If the goal is significant net growth, that process must be accelerated to launching two new missions annually for every one hundred existing churches. If the goal is to reach substantial numbers of younger generations and also new immigrants to the United States, a reasonable goal is three new congregations annually for every one hundred existing churches.

The common theme that runs through all of these examples is that life is a passing parade. The third-grade teacher in the local elementary school, the long-tenured pastor of a church, and the nurses in the hospital see this pattern over and over. It reminds one of the last lines in the motion picture *Grand Hotel:* "People come, people go. Nothing ever happens." As long as the replacements come along in adequate numbers, life appears to move on as usual. When the replacements coming along pick another manufacturer or retailer or brand name, however, the people in charge of the old institutions begin to display symptoms of anxiety.

The Ecclesiastical Scene

When we look at organized religion in North America, we see that same pattern. Every week approximately sixty-five Protestant congregations in the United States or Canada disband, merge into another church, dissolve, or simply fade away. That trend is offset by the fact that the average week also brings into existence well over 80 new congregations in the United States or Canada.

Likewise, the typical 500-confirmed-member Protestant congregation bids farewell to 25 to 50 members every year. If they are not replaced, that parish soon will discover it is growing older and smaller.

When we look more closely at that passing ecclesiastical parade, we see individuals, pastors, missionaries, teachers, leaders, congregations, parachurch organizations, theological seminaries, publishing houses, denominational agencies, authors, Christian colleges, and other institutions dropping out. Everyone, however, is replaced in one form or another, and the parade continues to grow larger. Nursing homes and cemeteries are filled with people once identified as irreplaceable. God continues to raise up both people and institutions for God's world. One evidence of this is that between 1970 and 1993 the total worship attendance in white Protestant congregations in the United States increased at a faster pace than the increase in the population.

In 1950 the predecessor denominations of what became the United Church of Christ, The United Methodist Church, the Christian Church (Disciples of Christ), and the Presbyterian Church (U.S.A.) included a combined total of 68,700 congregations. During the next forty years these denominations launched a combined total of at least 10,000 new congregations. The result in 1990 was that what are now four denominations reported a combined total of slightly under 59,300 congregations.

As that passing parade of Protestant congregations in the United States grew by more than 100,000 during those four decades, other religious bodies came forth to fill the vacuum created by the numerical decline of the long-established denominations. This can be illustrated by looking at four specific responses to filling that vacuum.

Four Responses to Changing Trends

Three of the most far-reaching developments of the second half of the twentieth century were (a) the decision by a dozen mainstream denominations to cut back sharply on their efforts in new church development, (b) a parallel decision to reduce the number of missionaries sent to other countries, and (c) the emergence of the Charismatic Renewal Movement.

Many denominational leaders ignored the Charismatic Renewal Movement. Others categorically rejected it. At least a few assumed it was a passing fad. A relatively small number embraced and affirmed it.

What happened next? One result was the planting of thousands of new congregations by independent churches, newer denominations, seminary professors, evangelistic-driven pastors, parachurch leaders, Spirit-filled Christians, and bivocational ministers.

A second result was the creation of literally thousands of independent Spirit-filled or Charismatic congregations.

A third was an increasing proportion of missionaries to other countries who were enlisted, sent, and supported by congregations not affiliated with any of the mainstream denominations. A fourth was the enlistment and credentialing of a new generation of pastors who were called to go out and plant new missions.

The Westward Movement

While rarely described in these terms, two significant factors behind many of these changes in that passing ecclesiastical parade are geographical facts of life. The first, and the most obvious, is that in 1940 40.4 million people, or 31 percent of the 132 million residents of the United States, lived west of the Mississippi River. A half century later, in 1990, the number of Americans living west of the Mississippi River had more than doubled to 97.2 million, or 39 percent of the population of the United States.

The second, and less frequently mentioned, pattern is that with the exception of the Lutheran Church-Missouri Synod, the Church of the Nazarene, and the Assemblies of God, nearly all the larger Protestant denominations have located their national headquarters east of the Mississippi River. Typically 60 to 75 percent of their congregations also are located east of that river.

The general pattern, of course, is that those religious bodies that trace their origins to the pre-Civil War era will have a large proportion of their congregations in the East, and most of their theological seminaries also will be in the East.

One result is that the newer denominations and the independent churches have had a major role in filling the resulting vacuum in the West.

One congregation that illustrates most of the points raised in this chapter traces its history back to March 3, 1977, when a group of Christians met for the first time at the Cortez High School

PROPORTION OF CONGREGATIONS WEST
OF
THE MISSISSIPPI RIVER 1990

American Baptist Churches	29%
AME Zion	6
Assemblies of God	57
Catholic Church	40
Church of the Nazarene	48
Christian Church (Disciples of Christ)	49
Church of God Anderson	33
Episcopal Church	33
Evangelical Free Church	62
Evan. Lutheran Church in America	44
Latter-Day Saints	83
Lutheran Church-Missouri Synod	54
Mennonite Church	19
Presbyterian Church (U.S.A.)	33
Presbyterian Church in America	18
Reformed Church in America	25
Seventh Day Adventist	47
Southern Baptist Convention	35
United Church of Christ	27
United Methodist Church	27
Wisconsin Evan. Lutheran Synod	43

in Phoenix, Arizona. These people came from thirty-four different religious traditions. They organized a new interdenominational, charismatic fellowship and named it Valley Cathedral. The following year they purchased the twelve-year-old set of buildings constructed earlier by the North Phoenix Baptist Church, which was relocating to a twenty-acre site a few blocks away. A new worship center was completed in early 1982.

The mission statement of this independent congregation includes these two key sentences: "The Valley Cathedral exists to go and make disciples at home and throughout the world . . . at the very heart of The Valley Cathedral is the desire to be a center of love, acceptance, and forgiveness within our community." A central theme of this congregation, which in early 1993 was averaging 2,800 at worship, is to serve as a *forgiveness* center, not a *guilt* center.

As part of the effort to fulfill that mission statement, this congregation not only offers regular weekly worship experiences and Bible classes, but it also operates a Christian day school for grades one-six, sponsors thirty-three missionaries, and has planted four new congregations in Maricopa County. It also sustains a network of six dozen home study groups in the Phoenix metropolitan area. Incidentally, all four of the pastors who planted those new congregations were reared in The Valley Cathedral. This congregation has filled several of the vacuums identified earlier in this chapter.

Another example of how an independent congregation moved in to fill the vacuum and meet the religious needs of new generations is Bethany Bible Church in Phoenix. This independent congregation planted at least ten new missions in the Phoenix metropolitan area. One of them, which traces its origins back to a couple of other factors, is the Scottsdale Bible Church. Founded in 1962, thirty years later it was averaging 3,500 at worship in two services on Sunday morning plus another 700 in children's church.

Despite the fact that it is now more than thirty years old, this congregation continues to seek to be responsive to the religious needs of new generations. One example is NightBreak. This is a casual Saturday evening experience designed for adults born after the mid-1950s. Two ministers and a lay volunteer spent eight months planning it before it was officially launched in the fall of 1991. One described it as an offbeat, Christian version of the NBC television program "Saturday Night Live." It is held in the church's gym and is designed around drama, laughter, live contemporary music, comedy, applause, informality, and fun. That is the context that opens the door—and the ears and eyes—of the three hundred participants to a brief but serious presentation of a basic Christian truth. Typically about half of those who come for this seventy-five minute experience are not members of this congregation.

NightBreak is not a typical Saturday evening worship service for church members who have to work Sunday morning or who will be out of town on Sunday. It is an event, an experience, a gathering, and an untraditional religious message. NightBreak is designed to reach young adults, and especially young single adults, who have no intention of attending any Sunday morning worship service anywhere. It is reinforced by "Wannabeland" scheduled concurrently for children up through grade three, by "The Big Idea" Sunday morning class for young adults, by "Daybreak," a Sunday morning young singles group, and by "Solos," a group for older single adults.

These two Arizona congregations illustrate five of the themes of this book. First, wherever a vacuum exists in responding to the religious needs of people, God lifts up a person or a group or a new institution to fill that vacuum. The decision by any one congregation or denomination "not to do that" does not mean it will not happen. Someone will come along to fill that vacuum.

Second, the Scottsdale Bible Church illustrates the fact that an effective means of reaching new generations is to design a new experience for a precisely defined slice of the population. Third, The Valley Cathedral illustrates that while many denominations are cutting back on planting new missions, that gap is being filled by congregations starting new churches.

Fourth, these two Arizona churches, and literally thousands of other Protestant congregations in North America, illustrate the rapid growth of independent or "nondenominational" churches. One reason for that growth is that many of today's independent megachurches have a systematic strategy for planting new missions. One example of this is Riverwood Community Chapel in Kent, Ohio. This "branch" of The Chapel in Akron met for worship for the first time on September 15, 1991. In 1992 worship attendance averaged 242. In the 1950s a new Protestant mission in Kent probably would have been initiated by local leaders affiliated with a mainstream Protestant denomination. Forty years later that initiative was taken by an independent megachurch twelve miles away. The vacuum continues to be filled. What has changed is the identity of the religious organization that fills it.

Fifth, the easiest and most effective means of responding to the religious needs of both newcomers to the community and new generations with new needs is to plant new congregations.

Finally, the more sensitive and the more carefully defined the response to the religious needs of people, the more likely people will come—but that is a subject worth a new chapter.

3.

IDENTIFY YOUR AUDIENCE

For several generations most congregations in American Protestantism have used one or more of the following nine criteria to define their constituency. For many immigrant congregations it was (1) language and national origins. For most of the others it was (2) denominational affiliation, (3) geographical proximity to the meeting place, (4) inherited loyalties through kinship ties, (5) social status ("that is the church for the movers or shakers in this town" or "that is a blue collar church"), (6) liturgy ("that is a low church Episcopal parish" or "that is an Anglo-Catholic parish"), (7) age ("that congregation serves an older clientele"), (8) theological belief system, or (9) polity.

The passing of time, the erosion of denominational loyalties, the popularity of the privately owned automobile, the huge public investment in excellent streets and highways, the change from a geographical to a nongeographical basis for meeting and making new friends, the emergence of a consumer-oriented society, the sharp drop in the number of immigrants coming to the United States from western Europe, the blurring of social class lines, and the increased affluence of the American people have made obsolete many of those organizing principles of yesteryear.

If the perspective is shifted to denominational strategies during the twentieth century, for most of that time four audiences motivated most of the work in launching new congregations. The clearest example was the effort by immigrant denominations to plant new congregations to serve the people coming from our common "home country."

A second pattern was "Our people are moving out there, so we have to start new churches to serve our people" (and to retain their allegiance to our denomination). This was especially common during the urbanization of America in the pre-1930 era and the suburbanization of America after World War II. During the past few decades, that also was a motivating factor for several denominations with most of their members residing north of the Mason-Dixon line and east of the Rocky Mountains to organize new missions in Florida, Georgia, Texas, Arizona, Colorado, the Pacific Coast, and other regions that were receiving thousands of migrants from the Northeast and Midwest.

A third audience that appealed to many denominational planners consisted of the first residents of new single-family homes.

More recently, many leaders from Protestant denominations that served a constituency that in 1975 was at least 95 percent white decided that the all-white denomination should become a multicultural, multiracial, multiethnic, and multilingual religious body. This decision meant the number-one audience for future new missions would be blacks, Hispanics, Asians, and other ethnic minority groups.

Largely overlooked in these denominational strategies to reach new audiences through new churches was that growing number of Americans who live in multifamily housing, in mobile home communities, in college and university dormitories, in luxury high rise apartments, and in nursing homes.

In 1960 approximately 15 million Americans lived in buildings that included five or more dwelling units. Thirty years later, that number had nearly tripled to 40 million. That is a big mission field!

What Does This Mean?

It is not a coincidence that the largest Protestant congregation in North America is also widely known for its skill in identifying a carefully and precisely defined constituency. This congregation, which held its first worship service in a motion picture theater in October 1975, also is the most widely studied church in North America, the most controversial, the most publicized, and the most copied.

From earliest days the leaders at Willow Creek Community Church in South Barrington, Illinois, have identified their constituency as "unchurched Harry and Mary," younger adults who display zero interest in the traditional offerings of conventional churches. Their approach to this constituency combines informality, drama, contemporary music, a thirty-five-minute sermon, theological conservatism, an exceptionally high-energy staff, an obsession with quality, an absence of traditional symbols, a low-pressure welcome to first-time worshipers, and an extensive range of outreach ministries.

The result has been that seventeen years after that first worship service, they were averaging nearly 15,000 in four weekend worship experiences designed for seekers, searchers, and others on a religious quest; the youth program was attracting over 4,000 teenagers every week; and that whole venture required the efforts of 4,500 volunteers. Most of the 7,000 members came from either an unchurched or a Roman Catholic background or both.

From this outsider's perspective, a persuasive argument can be offered that the distinctive characteristic of this large independent congregation is not its size or that high energy or the staff or that obsession with quality or their approach to the corporate worship of God. The unique characteristic is that week after week, year after year, and decade after decade, the number-one priority has been reaching that audience of unchurched adults. By year five, seven, or ten of their history, most new congregations have dropped evangelism to third or fourth place below (a) taking better care of their members, (b) real estate, and/or (c) money.

At the other end of the publicity and size scale is the Brunswick Reformed Church in Ohio. This congregation was founded in 1959 to reach newcomers to that exurban strip between Cleveland and Akron. For the next three decades it experienced the gradual numerical growth typical of many suburban missions founded in that era. In 1986, during the eighth year of service of the third and current pastor, the culture of the congregation was transformed. A motto was adopted, "Living His Love," which summarized the new culture. This new congregational culture was built on love, trust, and renewal. This congregation has been acting out meaningful responses to the four yearnings that Robert Randall contends people bring to the church.

1. **A yearning to feel understood.**
2. **A yearning to understand.**
3. **A yearning to belong.**
4. **A yearning for hope.**[1]

One of several ways this congregation has acted out meaningful responses to these yearnings is through renewal weekends. More influential, however, is that seven-day-a-week culture of love.

What has been the result of this transformation? One way to measure that is on the average worship attendance. For the decade 1977–87 worship attendance fluctuated between an annual average of 131 and 150. By 1992 it had doubled to 300. Even in sparsely populated exurbia there is a big audience for the congregation that is organized around God's love.

In 1980 the fastest growing Southern Baptist congregation in the country began with a home Bible study group of seven people in the Saddleback Valley section of Orange County, California. Rick Warren, the founding pastor, concluded that the people this new congregation should seek to reach and serve were symbolized by "Saddleback Sam." Saddleback Sam is a young urban professional who grew up in a home with some religious orientation, but no longer has ties to any worshiping community. Saddleback Sam is affluent, is self-satisfied, enjoys recreation, occasionally feels stressed out, and senses no need of any kind of organized religion.

After five hundred interviews with local residents, Warren concluded he had identified an evangelism target. He designed a strategy to reach Saddleback Sam that included nonjudgmental love, warmth, beginning with the other person's agenda, practical and positive sermons, a minimum of organizational structure, a strong emphasis on lay ministry, high quality and relevant advertising, openness, contemporary music, investing money in staff rather than in real estate in the early years, and a strong teaching ministry.

Rick Warren points out that the target audience for a church must be defined geographically, culturally, and spiritually as well as in terms of demographics and pyschographics. The more precisely your audience is defined, the easier it will be to reach, serve, and challenge your constituency.

What was the result of this effort to reach a narrowly and precisely defined audience? Fourteen years and 57 "temporary" meeting places later, this congregation was averaging 9,000 at worship and had just moved into its new permanent church home on a 74-acre site.

In addition to a precisely defined audience it was seeking to reach, the Saddleback Community Church possesses several other advantages. One is a determined, committed, energetic, visionary, and creative founding pastor who is still on the scene.

A second is a location in one of the fastest growing counties in the nation. The population of Orange County grew from 1.4 million residents in 1970 to 2.4 million in 1990. Orange County, however, is not a particularly hospitable environment for organized religion. During those twenty years, the reported membership of all Episcopal parishes in Orange County dropped by 15 percent, United Methodist membership plunged by 30 percent, the reported membership of the congregations affiliated with the Christian Church (Disciples of Christ) dropped by more than 40 percent, and the Presbyterian Church (U.S.A.) reported a 15 percent decline in membership. Rapid population growth does not make it easier for congregations to increase in size!

A critical asset at Saddleback Community was a mission statement that focused on the people, not on the institution. That four-part mission statement is consistent with the personal and spiritual journeys of many people. It begins with the need to attract and win people to Christ. This is followed by a recognition of the need to help people develop a Christ-like maturity. The third stage is to empower them for a meaningful ministry in the church. The fourth stage is to prepare these people to be involved in a life mission in the world in each stage and segment of their lives. Unlike most mission statements, that four-part articulation of purpose speaks directly and specifically to program planning.

At this point the reader may interrupt by adding, "It should be easy for a brand-new mission to identify an audience and a statement of purpose, but is that realistic for an old congregation with members who have been here for decades?"

That question has two answers. First, yes, it is easier for a new mission to identify a precisely defined audience. Second, while it is more difficult, yes, it also is possible for a long-established congregation to respond to a changing world by defining a new audience and accepting a new role.

An outstanding example of this is the First Presbyterian Church in Jamaica, a neighborhood in the Borough of Queens in New York City. It traces its origins back to 1662 when the Dutch still governed New Amsterdam. Two hundred and eighty years after it was founded, this was a large, relatively affluent, and influential congregation that included many of the leading families of that part of the city. It peaked in size with 1,628 members in 1951. Three hundred and ten years after it was founded, the active membership had dropped to one hundred. Most of the upper middle and middle class white families had moved away. Their replacements included large numbers of American-born blacks, plus immigrants from the Caribbean islands, Guyana, China, Africa, India, the Philippines, Latin America, Scotland, Puerto Rico, Canada, and Ireland.

By its three hundred and thirtieth birthday, this congregation had redefined its role as a "multi-ethnic, multi-racial, and multi-cultural congregation." It adopted a servant role in this larger community, emphasized shared leadership, redesigned corporate worship as a celebration of God's love, and affirmed diversity. It also must be added that this carefully defined redefinition of the audience resulted in an average worship attendance of over three hundred in 1993.

Yes, an old congregation can redefine its role, identify a new audience, and offer a meaningful response to the religious needs of that new audience.

One of the most controversial and divisive issues to confront several Protestant denominations in recent years is the relationship of that religious body to openly gay and lesbian adults. This issue has consumed huge quantities of time at the national denominational conventions, produced some heated rhetoric, and resulted in considerable national publicity in the secular media for that denomination. It also has resulted in limited constructive ministry, since most of these denominations are (a) too liberal in their theological position and (b) too rigid and legalistic in their polity to attract many churchgoing gays and lesbians. The greater the emphasis on the role of the denomination as a regulatory agency,[2] the greater the likelihood that the result will be alienation.

A completely different response to the issue of homosexuality, and one that also illustrates the value of defining an audience and carving out a distinctive niche is the Cathedral of Hope in

Dallas, Texas. This congregation, which is affiliated with the Universal Fellowship of Metropolitan Community Churches, traces its roots back to 1965 to a "circle of friends." Three years later the congregation was organized. Twenty-five years later, after meeting in a series of temporary locations, this congregation moved into its new $3 million building on a six-acre site near Love Field. With 900 members and another 1,000 constituents, this has become a megachurch that averages over 1,200 at worship and serves over 400 people living with AIDS.

Why did it grow so large? One part of the answer is the clear definition of three different audiences: (1) Christians who are self-identified gays and lesbians and have not been able to find any other churches that will openly accept and affirm them; (2) gays and lesbians with no active church affiliation; and (3) churchgoing parents of gays and lesbians who love their children and who have been frustrated by the rejection and hostility displayed by their home church to gays and lesbians. For some of these parents, their first experience with this rejection came when their adult child died from an AIDS-related illness and the pastor of their own church refused to conduct the memorial service. They turned to the Cathedral of Hope where they were greeted with love, sympathy, understanding, faith, acceptance, and support. Many of these older couples have decided to join this congregation.

Approximately 10 percent of the members are heterosexual. Men outnumber women at worship by a 3-to-2 margin.

The clearer and the more precise the definition of a congregation's audience, the easier it is to design a strategy to reach and serve that audience.

A sixth example of a congregation that began by defining an audience largely unreached by existing congregations takes a coffee break halfway through the Sunday morning worship service.

The 11,000 residents of the county seat town of Warsaw in northern Indiana have been well served by three United Methodist congregations with a combined membership of nearly 1,550. In

1990 the entire county included 65,000 residents and 23 United Methodist congregations. So why start a new mission there? After a year of trying to pioneer a "traditional" church with limited results, the decision was made that one more traditional church was not what was needed. In November 1991 the break was made. Tradition was replaced by an eight-piece band and contemporary Christian rock and jazz music. Within weeks, attendance nearly doubled from 60 to 110, and by early 1993 worship attendance was averaging 135. At that point it was larger than four-fifths of all United Methodist congregations in Indiana. The congregation has rented facilities in a local junior high school for a temporary meeting place, but has acquired a thirty-acre site east of town for a permanent church home.

Why did it work? Four reasons stand out. First, a clearly defined audience was identified. This consists largely of people born after 1963; some are married couples, others are divorced, and several have never married.

Second, the founding minister, born in 1960 and therefore one of the oldest adults in the congregation, soon recognized the need to be sensitive to the needs of the people rather than try to impose on them a predetermined agenda.

Third, corporate worship was designed to fit that generation of people and to offer a meaningful experience for them. The community gathers in the "commons room" of that school in an informal atmosphere. The twenty- to twenty-five-minute sermons bring the message of the Christian faith to such common concerns as fear, forgiveness, and parenting. That five-minute "fellowship and coffee break" halfway through the seventy-five-minute service reinforces both the informality and the focus in relationships and small groups.

Finally, since this is not a carbon copy of other churches in the area, it is not in competition with the others for new members. It may be a slight exaggeration to declare that the Celebration United Methodist Church represents a paradigm shift, but it is close.

4.

SIX PARADIGM SHIFTS

The phrase "paradigm shift" was first popularized by Thomas S. Kuhn in 1962.[1] In recent years it has become an overworked term, but it is the best available conceptual framework for introducing a half dozen changes in the context for doing ministry at the end of the twentieth century.

Who Takes the Initiative?

For much of the first two centuries of Protestant Christianity on the North American continent, the responsibility for initiating new ventures in ministry was divided by an ocean. One set of initiatives was taken by people in Europe. In North America the responsibility for new work rested largely on the shoulders of the clergy and secondarily on the laity. Several new religious organizations came into existence in the late eighteenth and early nineteenth centuries when a group of pastors came together and agreed to create what eventually became a denomination. By the eighteenth century, a significant degree of authority had been assigned to denominational agencies and offices. One historic example is the Plan of Union of 1801 in which the Presbyterians and Congregationalists agreed on a joint strategy for planting new congregations on the Western frontier.

The nineteenth century brought the emergence of denominations as powerful ecclesiastical agencies. Gradually much of the initiative that earlier had been lodged in congregations was delegated to denominational agencies and officials. The authority, power, and resources of most Protestant denominations reached a peak in the middle of the twentieth century. Thus nearly all of the leaders in denominational circles in the 1990s were people who had been born into a world in which denominations exercised great control. They were socialized into an ecclesiastical system in which the initiative for launching new ministries with new generations of people was assumed to be primarily a denominational responsibility.

The reality, however, changed during the last third of the twentieth century. Three developments fed this paradigm shift.

The first was the emergence of a remarkable variety of parachurch organizations that gradually began doing what denominations formerly did. That long list included enlisting, training, placing, and supporting people called to be missionaries in all parts of the world, resourcing congregations with a growing variety of materials, designing and administering continuing education experiences for both clergy and laity, assisting both congregations and regional judicatories in designing new strategies for mission, and counseling with congregations.[2] Much of what denominations once had monopolized now is being done by parachurch organizations. The two big exceptions are the certification and ordination of ministers and the administration of ministerial pension programs.

The second development was the arrival of a large new generation of exceptionally gifted, energetic, visionary, productive, and dedicated pastors born in the 1940–1960 era who built what today are commonly called megachurches. Many of these entrepreneurial ministers carried a strong denominational identity, and that megachurch continues to be a loyal member of the denominational family. Others were independent, and at least one-third of today's megachurches are not identified with any denomination. (See chapter 2.) The point of commonality, however, is that like the independent church, the leaders in these large denominationally affiliated congregations do not feel a need for help from the denomination. "They need us more than we need them" is a common description of the relationship.

More and more of these large congregations with substantial discretionary resources (primarily highly competent and deeply committed volunteers) feel both competent and comfortable in taking the leadership in initiating new ministries.

The third development was that many denominations discovered during the last third of the twentieth century that the demand on their financial resources exceeded their income. This limitation on financial resources reduced their ability to initiate new ministries.

Thus the first paradigm shift of the last third of the twentieth century has been and is the shifting of responsibility for initiating new ministries from denominations to large churches. The denominations are stuck with the responsibility for perpetuating yesterday and for certain institutional concerns, such as the operation of denominational agencies and pension systems, while those large congregations are free to take the initiative in giving birth to new ministries for a new day.

The Social Gospel Plus

At the beginning of the twentieth century, a Congregationalist minister by the name of Washington Gladden and a Baptist preacher, Walter Rauschenbush, popularized what eventually became known as the social gospel. By 1920, Protestants, Catholics, and Jews had all endorsed the belief that religious organizations should seek to reform society. As the decades rolled past, this thesis was expressed in four different forms. One was the prophetic voice calling for reform. A second was the delivery of social services to those in need. The third was to accept an active role as an advocate for social justice on behalf of the poor, the oppressed, the homeless, the hungry, the victims of discrimination including ethnic minorities, women, children, immigrants, persons with disabilities, the poor, and others. The fourth expression was the establishment of quotas to make sure all segments of the population were represented on both congregational and denominational committees, boards, and staff positions.

Tens of thousands of congregations actively acted out one or more of these four expressions of the social gospel. They established food pantries and clothes closets, they recruited volunteers to serve as advocates for those who needed that help, they opposed discrimination, and they cooperated with other congregations in delivering a huge range of social services.

The paradigm shift came with the addition of a radical concept. In addition to responding to the needs of the less fortunate, the delivery of those social services would include an effort to "congregationalize" the recipients. This strategy normally begins with identifying needs, responding to those needs, earning the right to be heard, Bible study, and, eventually, the creation of a new worshiping community. (See chapter 6.) Instead of hoping the recipients of these services will come and join our congregation on our turf, or at least read the tracts we hand out, the paradigm shift is to create a new indigenous worshiping congregation on their turf.

Clergy or Laity?

For some, the most radical of these six changes is the projection of greater expectations of lay volunteers. The old paradigm called for the clergy to initiate, to lead, to oversee, and to do. The new paradigm calls for greater responsibilities for the laity.

Most of the new models for ministry recognize that lay volunteers, not money, are the crucial resource in implementing new strategies for outreach. Instead of doing ministry, the clergy are being asked to identify, enlist, nurture, disciple, train, place, support, and resource teams of lay volunteers who will do the work. This shift offers renewed hope for those who dream of the ideal role of the minister as an enabler or facilitator. (This also may be the most demanding role for ministers in terms of vision, competence, creativity, leadership, dedication, strategy formation, hard work, long hours, faithfulness, and skill in interpersonal relationships.)

Collect Money and Regulate, or Strategy Formulation?

The fourth paradigm shift overlaps the first. In recent years several denominations have evolved into organizations with two distinctive responsibilities. One is the redistribution of wealth and income. Congregations with discretionary financial resources were asked to send money to denominational headquarters to be redistributed to congregations and agencies in financial need. The second was to serve as a regulatory body, to tell ministers, congregations, and church members what they could and should do and what they should not do.

This recent paradigm shift for denominations advances two new responsibilities to the top of the list. One is to accept a role in formulating strategies for new ministries in response to new needs and with new domestic mission fields. The second is to challenge congregations to be engaged in undertaking new forms of ministry and new ventures in outreach to respond to these needs.

Neighborhood or Regional?

The fifth of these six paradigm shifts may be the most controversial. Should congregations see themselves as neighborhood institutions or as regional churches? Is the appropriate model for the twenty-first century the neighborhood elementary school located in the middle of a large residential subdivision? Or is the Wal-Mart discount store a better model?

For several generations the standard answer, except for old First Church downtown, was the neighborhood school. Perhaps as many as one-fourth of today's Protestant churchgoers still prefer that approach to congregational life. Another one-fourth, however, place denominational affiliation above geographical convenience.

At least one-half of the churchgoers born after 1940, however, place quality, relevance, choices, and a meaningful response to their religious and personal needs above either geographical proximity or denominational label. They prefer the customer-driven Wal-Mart model.

Equally important, however, is another question. Which type of congregation can mobilize the extra resources required if that congregation is going to initiate several off-campus ministries? If the responsibility for initiating new ministries is passing from the denominations to congregations, which type of parish can accept and implement that role as a missionary church?

Today the answer appears to be that, with rare exceptions, it is the large, high-commitment, and outreach-oriented regional church.

How Do You Define *Church?*

Finally, the last of these changes is the most subtle. Should the word *church* be defined as a building or as a campus at a particular location? Or as a worshiping community of believers? Or should it be defined as a ministry without regard to any one meeting place? Or as one particular denomination? For example, can "one church" have two different meeting places? (See chapter 8.) Can it be a "church" if it does not carry a denominational affiliation?

A more common example is seen in those two church buildings across the street from each other. The bulletin boards in front now carry the same denominational identity. The two congregations trace their roots back to two different streams of American Protestantism, but several years ago a merger united those two streams into one denomination.

What is the next step? Should they compete as two congregations serving the same neighborhood? Or should they merge? Or should one relocate its meeting place to a site several miles away? Or should the two congregations merge administratively with one staff, one governing board, one budget, and one set of officers, but maintain two meeting places?

Or should they define their identity in ministry rather than by real estate? For example, one could accept a role as a tradition-driven congregation with liturgical worship and a pipe organ as the primary musical instrument, and seek to serve a regional constituency that prefers a traditional approach to the corporate worship of God. The other congregation could focus on a more informal and participatory approach to worship built around preaching, contemporary vocal music, a band, and a cafeteria of teaching experiences. It would seek to build a regional constituency of people seeking that approach to worship and the teaching ministry.

Or, in some traditions, one congregation could accept the role as an "evangelical" church and the other as the "liberal" church of that denomination in that town.

A third alternative would be for one to organize around missions in other parts of the nation and the world while the second would concentrate on building a network of off-campus ministries within twenty miles of the building.

In each case the definition of the word *church* would be around ministry, not real estate or "who goes there" or a denominational label.

While the reader need not agree that (a) these paradigm shifts do reflect contemporary reality or (b) they are significant for anyone looking ahead to the third millennium or (c) they have changed how we do ministry in the United States, it is necessary to understand two points. First, this observer believes that they do reflect a new reality. Second, at least an acknowledgment of all six is necessary to understand the Key Church Strategy and other new models of ministry described in the next five chapters.

5.

THE NEW PARTNERSHIP

The old systems are not working as effectively as they once did. That generalization applies to retailing, the practice of medicine, large public school systems, political parties, the Roman Catholic Church, labor unions, automobile manufacturing, universities, municipal police forces, agriculture, and dozens of other facets of American society. One of these is the operation of a large Protestant denomination.

Thanks to the advantages of a smaller scale, the absence of widespread anonymity, the cohesiveness that is enhanced by only one denominational theological seminary, a comparatively homogeneous belief system, the respect for tradition, the centrality of the parish ministry, a widely read denominational magazine, the high priority given to evangelism and missions, the lean denominational budgets, and a congregational polity, most of the smaller Protestant denominations in the United States have not encountered severe problems. The recent increase in the number of independent congregations described in chapter 2 means that a rapidly growing proportion of pastors and churchgoers are not worried about the future of their denomination. Why not? Because their church is not affiliated with a denomination. They may be a member of a coalition of congregations (or a coalition of individuals) organized around a particular cause, but they are not part of a denominational system.

On the other hand, at least one-third of the 350,000 Protestant congregations in the United States are affiliated with a denomination that clearly is confronted with serious problems. These problems usually include (1) the requests for money exceed the available financial resources; (2) the death rate among the members is rising, which is a sign of an aging constituency; (3) the number of members is shrinking; (4) the number of congregations that disappear each year from that denomination's roster exceeds the number of new congregations organized annually; (5) a growing alienation between the pastors and volunteer leaders in the parish and denominational officials that is evolving from apathy or indifference into an adversarial relationship begins to surface in denominational-congregational relationships; (6) the evolution of the role of the denomination from (a) mobilizing support for missions, (b) enlisting, screening, and credentialing clergy, and (c) resourcing congregations into the role of a regulatory body creates new points of tension over priorities; (7) points of conflict over cultural values begin to dominate the agenda at national conventions; (8) the erosion of institutional loyalties that once were transmitted from generation to generation have not been replaced by new organizing principles; (9) the emergence of a new era in religious music has surfaced as a divisive issue (a) between generations and (b) in congregational life; (10) the tendency to place the agenda of the clergy ahead of the needs of congregations is arousing more and more negative reactions among the laity; (11) the cost of the fringe benefits in a pastor's compensation package have increased far more rapidly since 1950 than the rate of increase in the income of the members, and this is pricing smaller congregations out of the ministerial marketplace; (12) a shift in power over decision-making from officially constituted denominational committees to self-appointed caucuses and lobbies creates new points of conflict; (13) the growing national distrust of centralized authority is reflected in "anti-headquarters" attitudes; (14) the growth of "consumerism" as a force in American society challenges the power of tradition; and (15) perhaps most significant of all but rarely discussed, the increased level of competition between new and/or relocated churches and long-established congregations for the next generations of churchgoers has jeopardized the future of many older churches.

This is far from a complete list of the problems, but it does illustrate why an increasing number of Protestant denominational leaders have concluded the old system is no longer working as effectively as it did in the first five or six decades of the twentieth century.[1]

What Are the Alternatives?

Given the number, size, and complexity of the problems facing each of several denominations, what can be done? How does a denomination respond to these and other problems? At least a dozen different responses have been offered on repeated occasions.

For many the favorite response was denial. Denial, however, is never a source of either hope or creativity, and the 1980s brought the demise of this response.

Far more constructive is the decision to begin with a careful, thorough, and systematic analysis of the new realities. An outstanding example of this was a research project undertaken by leaders in the Presbyterian Church (U.S.A.). This venture produced a seven-volume series, "The Presbyterian Presence: The Twentieth Century Experience," edited by Milton J. Coalter, John M. Mulder, and Louis B. Weeks, that stands out as a model for this response. It is filled with wisdom, candor, profound insights, relevant factual data, and constructive suggestions.[2]

For at least three decades the most attractive response was to seek to re-create an improved version of the 1950s. Unfortunately, no one yet has discovered how to re-create yesterday. A passive response accepted by many was to watch as the constituency grew older and smaller.

Others shrugged and declared the numerical decline was inevitable and used references to the decline in the number of farmers, steel workers, gasoline stations, and the defense industry as relevant parallels. "Some things just happen, and there is not much you can do to reverse the trend."

A few leaders accepted the role as cheerleaders and repeatedly called attention to the fact that the glass is not half empty, it is still half full. That can create an enthusiastic, supportive, and affirming audience for a few years, but when the glass becomes 60 percent empty, a few cynics recall the story about the emperor who wore no clothes in that famous parade.

A seventh response was to change the agenda by proposing a merger with another shrinking denomination. The results of the denominational mergers of the 1950–1990 era, however, have eroded much of the support for that alternative.

A few denominational leaders declared, "If congregations will send us more money, we can reverse our numerical decline." The growing credibility gap between congregational leaders and denominational headquarters has undercut the attractiveness of that appeal.

For at least a few, the most promising response was in expanding the role of the denomination as a regulatory body. If denominational officials could have a more influential voice in ministerial placement, in the staffing of congregations, in the allocation of scarce financial resources, in the planting of new missions, in the credentialing of the clergy, and in determining the priorities in missions, most of the problems could be solved. This alternative ran into difficulties when it was discovered that the number of people who were willing to be regulators greatly outnumbered those who wanted to be regulated. It also enhanced the attractiveness of the independent churches to the generations born after World War II.

A favorite of the 1970s and 1980s was to restructure the denomination in the hope of improving efficiency and reducing expenditures.

Another favorite was to deflect attention from the systemic issues by placing a controversial and divisive issue high on the denominational agenda and choosing up sides over that issue. Common candidates for that focal point were biblical interpretation, abortion, homosexuality, quotas, American foreign policy, health insurance for the clergy, racism, location of the denominational headquarters, and the role and status of women in the church.

A twelfth response was to identify a scapegoat. This always has great appeal and is a low-cost alternative. The prime candidates included the clergy, church members, theological seminaries, parachurch organizations, television, the megachurches, the secular media, the public schools, church-related colleges and seminaries, campus ministers, the military, and the federal government.

At this point the impatient reader may interrupt and demand, "Aren't there any positive and constructive responses on this list?" The answer is yes, there are at least four.

Four Positive Responses

One response was identified earlier. That is to begin with a careful analysis of contemporary reality based on high-quality research. The seven-volume series "The Presbyterian Presence: The Twentieth Century" stands out as an excellent model. This is *not* a plea for ancient history to be published as articles in academic journals. It is a plea for relevant research that sheds light on contemporary issues. This also is not a solution, only a beginning point.

A far more difficult possibility is to redefine the priorities and allocate at least three-quarters of all denominational resources (money and staff time) to (a) planting new congregations; (b) facilitating the emergence of additional large congregations that average seven hundred or more at worship since it is apparent that, when they perceive they have a choice, Americans born after 1955 clearly are choosing large churches in disproportionately large numbers; (c) resourcing existing congregations that are seeking to redefine their role in order to identify and reach new constituencies; (d) encouraging congregations to utilize television and other technological advances in reaching younger generations; and, perhaps most important of all, (e) helping congregations to improve the quality of their ministry.

This resourcing role for denominational agencies can and should be fulfilled in a manner that is both user-friendly and challenging, both responsive to the agendas of congregational leaders and also supportive of planned change, and both respectful of local traditions and open to new approaches to reaching new generations. That is not an impossible assignment! It has been accomplished by several regional judicatories.

A small but articulate and determined number of future-oriented leaders have identified a third alternative as the top priority for these troubled denominations. That is the identification, enlistment, training, screening, nurturing, apprenticing, and placement of the next generation of parish pastors. From the perspective of the year 2035, that probably will be the most influential product of what denominations do in the last years of the twentieth century and the first years of the third millennium. That, however, is a topic beyond the scope of this book.

A fourth response to the troubles of denominations is the subject of this book in general and the theme of this chapter in particular. This is to encourage a new partnership between that relatively small number of mission-oriented congregations with discretionary resources and the regional judicatory. One reason this alternative is so attractive is that the focus is on congregational outreach, missions, evangelism, and responding to the needs of people. A second is that in today's world, congregations, rather than denominational structures, appear to be the most effective vehicle for carrying out various forms of local mission. A third is that a working model of this new partnership has been invented, tested, and is in use by several dozen congregations. It is available for study, evaluation, and review. It can be adapted and implemented by any interested regional judicatory, or, in the smaller denominations, by the national home missions agency of that organization.

The Key Church Strategy

The history of this particular strategy for planned change can be traced back to the ministry of the First Baptist Church of Dallas, Texas. For several decades that historic downtown church has sponsored a couple of dozen off-campus ministries directed at people who could not or would not come to the building that was housing this congregation. From the earliest days, this congregation has been engaged in starting and maintaining new ministries in the Dallas area. These efforts include satellite Sunday schools and home Bible groups. These ministries were and are designed to reach a wide range of ethnic minority residents of Dallas as well as people in jails and prisons, people who are hearing impaired, and residents of large apartment structures. One of the newest efforts is to build a library of Christian books in every prison in Texas.

In 1977 The Baptist General Convention of Texas and Gambrell Street Baptist Church in Fort Worth decided to cooperate in launching new off-campus ministries. Gambrell Street Baptist Church had been organized in 1915. The original focus was to meet the spiritual needs of the students and staff of Southwestern Baptist Seminary, which was located in a sparsely populated area. As more people moved into that section of the city in 1928, the decision was made to expand that congregation's role as a neighborhood church. As more and more middle class Anglo-Americans moved in, the congregation grew in size. The average attendance in Sunday school grew to 923 in 1952. Twenty years later it was obvious that the future would not replicate the past. Sunday school attendance dropped by half as more and more working class Hispanics and Anglos moved into what had been a middle class neighborhood.

The congregation and the State Convention cooperated in a pioneering venture, later to be known as the "Key Church Strategy," to establish a series of indigenous satellite churches and missions in that section of Fort Worth. (It should be noted that the term *Key Church* was first used as part of the Southern Baptist Convention's Home Mission Board strategy called the Bold Mission Thrust.)

This cooperative venture between the State Convention and the Gambrell Street Church succeeded and became the model for others to study and adapt to their own circumstances.

A Four-Point Strategy

By 1992 Gambrell Street Baptist Church's outreach ministries included four types of off-campus ministries.

1. Eight church-type missions (Nigerian, two African American, middle class Anglo, two Hispanic, Japanese, and one working class Anglo) with a combined membership of 499.

2. Indigenous Satellite Churches (House Churches). Nineteen of these had been started, and seven with a combined membership of 145 were still in existence in 1991. Five of the seven were working-class Anglo missions.

3. Multihousing Missions created to serve residents of apartment complexes. At the end of 1991 Gambrell Street Baptist Church was sponsoring seven of these missions with a combined average attendance of 155. They also had helped to start four others that now are sponsored by other congregations.

4. Mission Ministries that are not able to evolve into autonomous worshiping communities. These usually are located in institutional settings such as nursing homes, prisons, drug rehabilitation centers, and hospitals. At the end of 1991 that list included six missions with a combined average attendance of 166.

What has happened at the Gambrell Street Baptist Church since beginning to implement this outreach strategy? The average attendance of the core congregation peaked at 923 in 1982 and was down to 474 in 1991. Attendance at all of the off-campus ministries averaged 109 in 1980, 257 in 1982, and 608 in 1991. In seven of the ten years, 1982–1991 inclusive, the combined attendance averaged over 1,000 for the core congregation and these off-campus ministries.

More significant than these statistical comparisons, however, are four other products of this effort, (1) the baptism of scores of new converts to the Christian faith, (2) the new set of relationships between this Anglo congregation and the newer residents in that community, (3) a meaningful outreach to Hispanics, African Americans, and other ethnic minority groups, and (4) a retention of that high priority on missions at Gambrell Street Baptist Church—in similar circumstances so many other congregations replace their missional outreach with survival goals.

On the downside, the core congregation at the mother church is growing older, smaller in numbers, and more isolated from the local community.

Second, only two of all of those missions have reproduced by starting new missions—but together they have launched ten new missions. That is far fewer than the dream called for, but when compared to the number of new missions started during the past dozen years by the typical association, diocese, presbytery, synod, conference, or district, that total does not call for an abject apology!

Out of that early partnership with Gambrell Street Baptist Church, the Baptist General Conference of Texas has evolved the Key Church Strategy.[3]

The heart of this strategy is that the regional judicatory challenges larger mission-minded congregations to initiate new off-campus ministries. This makes it possible for the denominational agencies to allocate more resources to planning, to formulating strategies to reach precisely defined segments of the population, to offer training events for both paid staff and volunteers in ministry, and to sharply expand the total scope of these outreach endeavors.

What Does This Mean?

What are the criteria for acceptance into this partnership? Every regional judicatory must answer that question for itself and tailor its response to fit the local circumstances. The Baptist General Convention of Texas defines a Key Church as one that meets these six criteria:

1. Makes a long-term commitment to make missions outreach a top priority.

2. Prioritizes missions to the level of the church's religious education and music programs.

3. Establishes a Missions Development council.

4. Elects a director/minister of missions to lead missions expansion.

5. Begins five mission/ministry units each year.

6. Sponsors at least five dependent or pre-independent satellite units on a continuous basis.[4] Each regional judicatory must define the criteria that are consistent with its strategy, goals, values, and resources.

Four Fringe Benefits

From this observer's perspective, the Key Church Strategy also offers several significant fringe benefits.

The most obvious is that this can be a powerful influence in the revitalization of the long-established and self-centered congregation that has moved care of the members and care of the real estate to the top of the local list of priorities in the allocation of resources.

Second, in an era when the relationships between denominational agencies and the leaders of large and growing congregations in that denomination frequently have been evolving from cooperative to apathetic to hostile to adversarial, the Key Church Strategy can be a productive means of building a new cooperative partnership between the regional judicatory and those congregations.

Third, in a day of scarce financial resources in most denominational agencies, this is a productive strategy for expanding ministry. Vision and volunteers, not money, represent the critical resources for this partnership in mission. Money frequently follows vision and volunteers.

Fourth, and most important, for those who agree that one of the primary reasons for the existence of worshiping communities is to transform lives, the Key Church Strategy is a proven method of doing that. The lives of the volunteers are transformed. The lives of many of the people being ministered to are transformed. The lives of the key church leaders are transformed. This is a transformational strategy.

How can this new partnership be adapted to expand the ministry of your congregation and of your denomination? Can it be adapted for use by independent or nondenominational churches?

Three different answers to those questions are introduced in the next three chapters, but before looking at those operational alternatives, it may be wise to examine several of the assump-

tions on which this strategy is based. If you cannot affirm the
assumptions, you may not want to adopt the strategy!

Crucial Assumptions

The Key Church Strategy offers tremendous promise for every
denomination prepared to redefine its role in the twenty-first
century. The critical distinction in describing it, however, is that
it is not a program. It is not a Band-aid. It is not a proposal for
reform. It is not a means of perpetuating the status quo. It is a
strategy for change.

Because it is a strategy for change, not a program, the best
introduction to it is a review of some of the assumptions this
observer believes are the foundation for an effective implementation of the concept.

One of the fundamental assumptions is that every human
being is a child of God, a person of worth, and that every
individual has been endowed with God-given gifts.

Equally important is the assumption that the call to salvation
also is a call to service.

This strategy is based on the assumption that congregations
and volunteers can be trusted. Thus it may not be a relevant
strategy in those religious traditions organized on the basis of
distrust of congregations and of lay volunteers. Central to this
strategy is the assumption that every outreach ministry should
be expected to create a new worshiping community. That may
not always be the result, but that is an expectation.

That expectation is undergirded by the assumption that indigenous leadership is essential to the creation of a self-governing,
self-financing, self-expressing, and self-propagating Christian
community. This assumption means the strategy may not be
appropriate for those religious traditions that display substantial
distrust of indigenous leaders.

This assumption represents the biggest break with the traditional social justice and social services ministries. These tradi-

tional outreach ministries are based on the assumption that those with resources should help those without resources. Feeding the hungry, sheltering the homeless, caring for the sick, and providing homes for children, the elderly, the poor, pregnant young women, the terminally ill, or the handicapped are examples of this traditional approach. It often began and ended with providing help.

One of the price tags on this traditional approach has been that it reinforced a sense of helplessness by the recipients of the services. It encouraged the disadvantaged to an increased level of dependency on outside help.

The Key Church Strategy affirms social services and advocacy as good beginning points, but only as beginning points. This strategy recognizes, affirms, and seeks to develop the inherent worth of individuals by empowering them to participate *and to lead* in building new Christian communities. This strategy assumes that many of these off-campus ministries can and should lead to "congregationalizing" those in need and challenging them to become disciples of Jesus Christ. Among other things, this means that indigenous leadership development is a pivotal component of this strategy. The delivery of social services and the role of the advocate is always accompanied by the gospel.

Instead of wondering "why those people who live so close to our church don't come here"—and most of them won't as long as we identify them as "those people"—the Key Church Strategy is based on the assumption that "we" have a New Testament call to carry the gospel to other people on their turf and to take the church to the people. An overlapping central assumption of this strategy is that with some people *hearing* the gospel will transform their lives, with others the *study* of the Scriptures is the crucial beginning point in this transformational process, but with many the critical beginning point is for someone to *hear and respond* to their individual and personal needs.

For many traditionalists one of the most difficult assumptions to accept is that the church is people, not a building. In several religious traditions an equally threatening assumption is that lay volunteers may be more effective in certain outreach ministries than are the seminary-trained clergy.

Another assumption that separates the Key Church Strategy from many traditional mission programs is that sending money is not the primary resource. The number-one resource to be mobilized by these churches consists of volunteers, not money.

Another assumption is that long-term financial subsidies may undermine efforts to create self-governing, self-supporting, self-propagating, and self-expressing congregations.

For those who have operated on the principle that the top priority in congregational life is care of the members, the most challenging assumption of the Key Church Strategy is that missions must become a long-term high priority for that particular congregation. This means raising missions to the same level of importance in the allocation of resources as the Sunday school, the ministry of music, and youth programing. Operationally this means that the congregation with a senior pastor, a minister of music, a director of Christian education, and a youth minister must add the position of minister (or director) of missions to the table of organization and include in the budget an adequate amount of money for local missions.

In many congregations the primary responsibility of the missions committee or a missions council is to mobilize financial support for missions. The Key Church Strategy calls for a far larger role. The primary task of the missions council is not raising money; it is identifying unmet needs and missional opportunities, formulating a strategy to respond to these opportunities, and enlisting volunteers to be actively engaged in doing ministry. It is difficult to accomplish this without the help of either (a) a volunteer director of missions or (b) a paid minister of missions.

This raises what some will identify as the critical variable in the adoption and implementation of the Key Church Strategy. The pastor or the senior minister must be unreservedly and completely supportive of this priority in the life and ministry of that congregation. If the senior pastor (or the newly arrived successor) is not fully supportive of this high priority for missions, it probably will soon encounter serious difficulties.

One of the more subtle assumptions on which the Key Church Strategy rests is that many congregations do have discretionary resources. The congregation that allocates all of the time and energy of all of the potential volunteers for maintaining that church's program and does not believe it possesses discretionary resources probably should ignore the Key Church Strategy.

While it is not always publicly stated this bluntly, one assumption is that high-commitment congregations are more likely to seek to join this partnership than are low-commitment churches.

For those who believe strongly in the value of the permanency of religious institutions, one of the assumptions behind the Key Church Strategy may be difficult to accept. Not all of these new off-campus outreach ministries endure forever. Many exist for only a year or two. At least a few may disappear after only a few weeks or a couple of months. Examples of short-lived ministries include the summer backyard Bible study program for children, some of the house churches, and a fair number of adult study groups.

In several Protestant traditions one of the potentially divisive assumptions concerns rituals, ordinances, and sacraments. What can be done in these off-campus ministries? Can baptisms be performed at these off-campus locations? Weddings? Can Holy Communion be served in an off-campus setting? Can people be received into membership in the core or sponsoring congregation at these off-campus locations? Or must people come to the sponsoring congregation's meeting house to participate in one or more of these religious acts?

For some of the leaders the most surprising assumption is the recognition of the need for a continuing educational program within the sponsoring congregation. This usually is the responsibility of the minister of missions. This means a never-ending effort to inform, inspire, and challenge the members about the need to keep mission outreach alive and a top priority. In simple terms, this effort is based on the assumption that the natural, predictable, and normal tendency in all worshiping communities is for institutional maintenance and care of the members to move to the top of the agenda.

While rarely stated, one assumption is that the volunteers most likely to come forth to implement this strategy are people who have experienced the transforming power of the gospel in their own lives. The expectation is that the lives of these volunteers will be enriched and some will have their lives transformed.

One of the most controversial issues to come out of the Church Growth Movement is the "homogeneous unit principle." This statement simply recognizes the tendency for people who share similar characteristics to socialize with one another. It is most highly visible in the lunchrooms of large high schools, in retirement communities, in bars, in adult Sunday school classes, in Protestant congregations, and in other voluntary associations. This principle explains why long-established congregations tend to attract as new members people who resemble the current membership. This predictable human tendency has been denounced by those who are convinced that every worshiping community should be a multicultural, multiracial, and multiethnic gathering. That goal is difficult to attain. One alternative is to organize a relatively small congregation around a network of one-to-one relationships. At the hub of that network is a long-tenured pastor with a high level of competence in building one-to-one relationships with people who come from a huge variety of social, educational, ethnic, racial, cultural, economic, and vocational backgrounds. As the members begin to identify one another as individuals, rather than as representatives of a "tribe," as acquaintances become friends, as they work together on shared missional goals, and as this network of one-to-one relationships is reinforced by that skilled pastor, a remarkably heterogeneous congregation often emerges.

A second alternative is to bring people from highly diverse backgrounds together around a common goal. One such common goal is salvation. Another is the baptism of the Holy Spirit. Another is strong upwardly mobile ambitions for "our children," and the operational expression of this is the creation and operation of a Christian day school.

A third alternative is to create a high-commitment congregation that projects comparatively high expectations of every member. The Seventh Day Adventists and the Church of Jesus Christ of Latter-day Saints (Mormons) are two contemporary examples of this model.

A fourth alternative is the Key Church Strategy. A central component of this strategy is that a relatively homogeneous congregation can reach and be engaged in ministry with a widely diverse collection of people through off-campus ministries. Instead of simply sending money to help fund the creation of new homogeneous congregations that may reach a different slice of the population, the Key Church Strategy is based on the assumption that by sending both people and money, and by initiating new off-campus ministries, the upper middle class Anglo congregation can be engaged in doing ministry with people from a huge variety of cultural, racial, ethnic, social class, economic, and vocational backgrounds.

While this is far from a comprehensive summary of the assumptions on which the Key Church Strategy is based, they are presented here for four reasons.

First, this is one means of explaining the religious culture on which this strategy rests.

Second, these assumptions offer guidelines for those congregational leaders who ask, "Is this an appropriate strategy for us to adopt?" In many cases local traditions, the polity, or the demands of this strategy suggest the appropriate answer is "No, this is not for us."

Third, these assumptions provide a simple means for distinguishing this concept from other missional strategies.

Finally, and perhaps most important, one means of minimizing future surprises, conflicts, and problems in implementing any missional strategy is for all the leaders responsible for designing and implementing it to begin by defining and agreeing on the underlying assumptions.

How Do We Begin?

Is the Key Church Strategy a model for missions that can and should be adopted by your congregation or your denomination? If the answer is in the affirmative, the first step may be for your policy makers to examine these assumptions. Are you comfortable with them? Are you comfortable with the need to shift control out of the denominational structure and encourage a partnership between the denomination and congregations in designing and implementing an outreach strategy? Many will insist it is easier for congregations to act unilaterally, while others will contend that it is more effective if the denomination has complete control over initiating new missions and new ministries.

A logical second step is to launch a pilot project or two. Identify a couple of congregations that already place a high priority on missions, that possess the discretionary resources required for implementation of this strategy, and that display a venturesome spirit. An essential requirement is the enthusiastic and unreserved support of the pastor or the senior minister. Three other critical resources are (a) a strong future orientation, (b) a cadre of deeply committed lay volunteers who will commit themselves to four to five hours of ministry every week, and (c) a training program for both the volunteers and that congregation's minister of missions.

While this may not be required for every subsequent key church that is enrolled in this strategy, the first couple of pilot projects should be overseen by a full-time paid minister of missions who is a staff member of that key church. In some congregations the pastor or some other staff person may serve as the part-time minister of missions and occasionally a volunteer will be the best choice.

The regional judicatory of the sponsoring denomination may offer to pay part of the compensation for that new staff position for the first year or two as part of that judicatory's long-term strategy for enlisting key churches.

That minister (or director) of missions will carry the primary staff responsibility for (a) organizing and staffing a missions council that will identify potential off-campus ministries; (b) enlisting, training, placing, supporting, and working with the volunteers who will be engaged in doing ministry; (c) working with that regional judicatory on issues of priorities, funding, staffing, and launching new outreach ministries; (d) designing and implementing a continuing education program to keep the members and leaders of that congregation well informed about the progress of this mission strategy; (e) achieving the goal of launching at least five new missions or outreach ministries annually; (f) overseeing the progress of each of these new ministries; (g) recommending when a particular new worshiping community should be encouraged to take that critical step of becoming an autonomous self-governing, self-funding, self-expressing, and self-propagating congregation; (h) suggesting how a specific new work should be terminated; (i) working with a subcommittee of the missions council on the preparation of a budget for the coming fiscal year; and (j) working with the missions council in identifying additional opportunities for new outreach ministries for next year.

To add that set of responsibilities to a person currently on the staff is somewhere between unrealistic and prescriptive of failure. The sixth or seventh congregation in that regional judicatory to sign up as a key church may decide to begin with a volunteer director of missions who will be trained in and by one of the pilot churches that has two or three years of success with this strategy. It is strongly advised, however, that the first two or three congregations in any regional judicatory that volunteer to pioneer the Key Church Strategy in that judicatory should have the services of a full-time minister of missions.

The first large-scale effort by any other denomination to replicate the Key Church Strategy was launched in 1992 by the North Texas Conference of The United Methodist Church. The leaders in this annual conference have recognized that this strategy can be an effective means of reaching people who live in multifamily housing, in mobile-home communities, and in lower socioeconomic neighborhoods with the gospel of Jesus Christ. Their implementation plan calls for a strong emphasis on training, a large role for bivocational ministers, and the expectation that each key church will launch five new missions annually.

How Do We Pay for It?

While the four crucial resources for implementation of this strategy are a commitment to missions, a cadre of deeply committed volunteers, visionary and skilled leadership, and a positive future orientation, sooner or later money will be needed.

One possibility is to finance it through the congregational budgeting processes. A second is a partial subsidy from the regional judicatory of that denomination. Both of these channels often have low ceilings.

A third possibility, which often does not have such a low ceiling over it, is designated second-mile contributions. Missions is the most appealing cause for raising money. Unless this conflicts with local policies, a special financial appeal may be the best means of funding the Key Church Strategy. The stronger the commitment of the members of that congregation to local missions, the greater the chances the Key Church Strategy will be successful. Likewise, the stronger the commitment of the members to local missions, the easier it will be to fund that strategy through designated giving.

A compatible and complementary fourth possibility is to organize one or more 501(c)3 corporations that will be responsible for implementation of certain phases of the larger strategy. (See item 22 in chapter 1.)

A one-time fringe benefit of designated second-mile contributions is to speed up the process. One reasonable goal would be that the compensation package for a full-time staff person to serve as minister of missions could be funded for that first year through a special financial appeal. A second goal is that three months after the new missions council comes into existence, a second financial appeal could raise the money necessary to fund those new outreach ministries for the next twelve months. Funding that new staff position and the first year's budget through the regular congregational budgeting process might require ten to eighteen months more time than would these two special appeals.

How Many?

How many congregations will come forward to accept this role as a key church? It is far too early to offer a definitive answer to that question, but four statements can be made with a high level of confidence. First, at least 90 percent of all the congregations in any regional judicatory cannot or will not become a part of the implementation of this strategy.

Second, if ten years after adopting this missions strategy a regional judicatory can report that 2 percent of all congregations are active as key churches, that should be seen as an excellent response. A response rate of 3 percent can be classified as a middle-sized miracle. If the report states that 10 percent of all congregations in that regional judicatory currently are active as key churches, that probably means (a) there is a problem with the definition of terms or (b) someone is misrepresenting the facts.

Third, and far more important, if as many as one percent of the congregations in any regional judicatory commit themselves to implementing the Key Church Strategy, that probably will double, triple, or quadruple the amount of new outreach ministries launched in that conference, association, synod, diocese, or region in any one year.

Fourth, accepting the role as a key church can be an influential component of a larger strategy for enhancing the vitality, life, and ministry of any congregation.

What Happens Next?

To open the doors to the next stage of this discussion, let us assume that (a) your regional judicatory has decided to adopt this concept as the heart of the local mission strategy; (b) three different congregations, each with the enthusiastic and unreserved endorsement of the senior minister, have come forward to serve as the first key churches in this regional judicatory; (c) each one has brought to the staff a full-time minister of missions; and (d) newly created missions council will meet for the first time tomorrow night. (In one of these three congregations the missions council was organized earlier and began its work by serving as the committee to search for the person to fill that newly created position of minister of missions.) What happens next?

Do you want to launch new off-campus ministries to reach people who will not come to your meeting place? Or will your beginning point be to go to the assistance of some of the "wounded birds" who no longer can fly by themselves? Or has the time come to consider the multisite option? If you are comfortable with the assumptions stated earlier, the next three chapters elaborate on these alternatives.

6.

OFF-CAMPUS MINISTRIES

Thousands of Protestant congregations in the United States trace their origins back to the day when a group of laypersons from old First Church downtown came out and organized a Sunday school for children. Eventually that mission grew into a self-governing, self-financing, self-expressing, and self-propagating congregation.

During and after World War II many large urban congregations sent their associate minister, along with a cadre of volunteers, to pioneer a new congregation out on the edge of the suburban frontier. Once again it was expected that these missions would grow into autonomous and self-supporting congregations. This strategy is still followed by many in that growing number of independent churches.

In several denominations, however, the next stage was to shift this responsibility from congregations to the regional judicatories and/or national agencies of that religious organization. Congregations were asked to send money to the denomination to finance a strategy for new church development. In several traditions a multimillion dollar capital funds campaign was launched by denominational leaders to help fund these church-planting efforts.

As the denominational emphasis on starting new missions was replaced by a concern about the inner city during the 1960s, congregations were asked to send money to denominational headquarters to help finance these ministries. Subsequently an expanded emphasis on issue-centered ministries brought calls for additional funds. Many congregations, and at least a few denominational leaders, evaluated a congregation's support of missions, not by the number of missionaries or volunteers who came from that parish, but rather by the increases in the number of dollars sent to denominational headquarters.

More recently the changing nature of American society has surfaced needs that are beyond the resources of denominational agencies, so new strategies have been designed. One is the Key Church Strategy described in the previous chapter. Before examining a few of these new strategies and new models of ministry, however, it may be useful to look at four other facets of this subject.

Who Are the Target Audiences?

One reason for the emergence of new models is that the old strategies were not able to reach an increasing number of segments of the population. These "hard-to-reach" populations have grown to a long, long list. That list includes commuter students enrolled in institutions of higher education; adults in jails and prisons; residents of mobile-home courts; recent immigrants from Mexico, Central and South America, Asia, Africa, and the Caribbean Islands; low-income households; visitors to state and national parks; one-person households; undergraduates living in college and university dormitories; single-parent families; people who spend the weekend on their boat or at the marina; winter visitors in the Sunbelt; Americans born in the 1969–80 era; divorced men; residents of nursing homes; delinquent teenagers in state-operated corrections institutions; families who go to their cottage at the lake or in the mountains nearly every weekend during the summer; tourists; the homeless, and residents of the luxury, high-rise apartment towers in the central city. Many of these people can be reached with the gospel of Jesus Christ only through off-campus ministries. They do not come to our traditional church buildings.

Have you identified the target audiences your congregation expects to reach during the next ten years? Do you believe this can be accomplished by inviting them to come to your meeting place? Or will it be necessary to launch off-campus ministries to reach some of them?

The Crucial Distinction

What is the difference between this approach to off-campus ministries and such traditional ventures as the rehabilitation of housing in the inner city or opening a soup kitchen on skid row or providing a chaplain for a local four-year liberal arts college or conducting worship services early every Sunday morning out at that lake surrounded by cottages and tents or enlisting members to serve as tutors in a public school in a poverty neighborhood eight miles away or leading a Sunday afternoon worship service at the local nursing home or sending food, money, and volunteers to staff a food pantry in the inner city or building and operating a high-rise apartment building designed to house senior citizens or visiting inmates in the nearby state prison?

As was pointed out in the preceding chapter, the crucial difference is the expectation that every one of these off-campus ministries will evolve into a continuing worshiping community.

As you design your ministry plan for the twenty-first century, will you build your outreach strategy simply around helping others or do you expect those efforts also will result in the creation of new worshiping communities? That is a crucial distinction in planning a strategy for a new day!

Two Different Beginning Points

Among the many operational responses to that growing number of hard-to-reach people, eight can be summarized by these frequently heard statements.

"Everybody knows apartment dwellers don't go to church."

"When those young people grow up, marry, settle down, and have children, they'll be back in church."

"We're here; our doors are open, our members are friendly, and we welcome strangers. If anybody is looking for a new church home, we'll be glad to see them."

"There are some people that you can't reach, no matter what you do."

"Our first obligation, as a congregation, is to the people who founded this church and sacrificed to make it what it is today."

"Let's go door-to-door and call on everyone who lives within a mile of our building and invite them to come and worship with us next Sunday."

"With the crime rate going up the way it is, we need to light our parking lot, buy a security system for the building, and hire guards for whenever we have night meetings."

"Let's face it; this church is designed to reach only one class of people, so let's relocate our meeting place to a site where we can reach people like us."

All eight of these responses are based on a common assumption. That assumption is that our ministry depends on people coming to our meeting place. That is the beginning point for designing an operational strategy.

The theme of this chapter, and a central thread for this book, is that a more productive strategy begins with going to the people, meeting them on their turf, and beginning with their agenda.

That is *not* a new idea. The best model can be found in the New Testament in the ministries of Jesus, Paul, and others. United Methodists, of course, will point to John Wesley and to that army of circuit riders of the eighteenth and nineteenth centuries as legitimizers of this strategy for their denomination.

As you design the ministry plan for your congregation for the twenty-first century, are you basing your evangelistic strategy on the assumptions that people will come to your meeting place or that you will have to go to them?

Two Other Forks in the Road

Should the new ministries to be launched to reach these various segments of the population be initiated by denominational agencies or by congregations? What is the primary responsibility of congregations? To initiate new off-campus ministries? Or to send money so this can be done by denominational agencies? In some denominations both polity and recent traditions make it clear that the primary responsibility of congregations is to send money. In other Protestant bodies that is still an open question.

If the decision is that congregations should be encouraged to initiate new off-campus ministries, that brings us to a second fork in the road. Should these off-campus ministries be staffed by paid specialists? Or by volunteers? Should we hire a minister to plant a new congregation in that complex of three hundred apartment units a half mile from our building? Or should we staff it with volunteers?

The best answer to those questions may be yes. Our congregation will add a part-time or full-time minister of missions to our staff who will help design the strategy, oversee the implementation of that strategy, enlist, train, place, and support the network of volunteers required to staff it and to help identify new opportunities in missions and outreach.

Off-Campus Apartment Ministries

Is this a dream of what could be done in an ideal world? Or can it really work? The answer is that it can work. It is being done. Perhaps the best place to begin is to look at the experiences and learnings of those who have been doing it in apartment ministries.

In 1993 the housing inventory of the United States included approximately 64 million detached single-family homes, nearly 7 million attached single-family houses, 10 million units in buildings with 2-to-4 dwelling units, 21 million apartments in buildings with five or more units (15 million of these were in structures with 10 or more units), and nearly 8 million mobile homes. Approximately two-thirds of all dwelling units were single-family homes.

Well over 7 million of those housing units were occupied by single-parent mothers with children under 18 at home.

These statistics reveal why (a) the housing industry is heavily oriented toward construction of single-family homes and most churches concentrate their program and ministries on reaching people living in single-family homes—after all, three-quarters of the construction dollars go for one-family homes—and (b) nearly three-quarters of the American population live in single-family houses. (In 1990 nearly 2 million Americans lived in college dormitories, 1.8 million in nursing homes, 1.1 million in correctional institutions, and 600,000 in military housing.)

If most Americans live in single-family homes, and if those are the people our church is most effective in reaching and serving, why change? Don't fix what isn't broken!

One response to that is the fact that in mid-1993 60 million Americans were living in apartment buildings of all sizes, and another 12 million resided in mobile homes. That is 72 million, the equivalent of the total population of the United States one hundred years ago.

A second response is the Great Commission (Matthew 28:19-20).

A third reason is that we now know how to do it. One of the wisest and most effective pioneers in creating congregations in large multifamily apartment communities is Barbara Oden.

How Do You Do It?

Barbara Oden, who may be the nation's number-one expert on apartment ministries, declares, "Give me two volunteer couples and $100 a month, and we can start an apartment ministry anywhere you choose." The credibility behind that statement is the record. She has done it over and over again. In 1986, after eight years as an apartment manager, Barbara accepted the challenge to start a ministry in the Springbrook Village apartments.

In 1990 she moved to the staff of the Union Baptist Association in Houston. Three years later, 58 churches in that Association were operating 92 off-campus ministries.

What is the secret of these ventures?

First, begin with the apartment manager, superintendent, or owner. "How can we make your life easier and better?" can be the best opening question.

The next step is a face-to-face survey of the residents to identify their needs. In many it is a need for lessons in English as a second language. In one apartment community, dozens of single-parent mothers had difficulties with their cars. A crew of volunteer automobile mechanics, a few professional but most amateur, helped to get most of those cars in better condition. In many, the need is to bring in volunteers to staff an activities program. Male volunteers from the Key Church may come to watch Monday night football in the community room with the men and youth living in the apartments. That can open doors. Many newcomers to the United States need help with the immigration authorities or they need help in grocery shopping or in going to the health clinic to have their children vaccinated. After-school activities for children and Saturday programs almost always are popular. The list of needs is endless.

As the volunteers from the Key Church address these needs, credibility is established. As the needs of the residents are met, the turnover rate drops, vandalism is less common, new friendships develop—and the life of the apartment manager becomes a little easier. The self-confidence and skill of the volunteers improve.

After that right to be heard has been earned, it usually is possible to expand the program to include adult Bible study, crafts, Sunday school classes for the children, and a vacation Bible school. Indigenous leaders begin to be identified and emerge from the group. Eventually a resident may ask, "Would it be possible for us to have church here?"

Concurrently, the trained volunteers from the sponsor church are (1) being uplifted by the prayer support of the people in their home congregation, (2) maintaining contact with the apartment manager and being sensitive to the feelings and agenda of the manager, (3) identifying other needs they can address, (4) keeping the door open to the leading of the Holy Spirit, (5) enjoying the participation in a support group consisting of fellow volunteers engaged in similar ministries in other places, (6) getting their questions answered by the Minister of Missions, (7) training indigenous future leaders, (8) becoming increasingly involved in the lives of other people far more quickly and deeply than they had ever thought possible, (9) feeling frustrated when the needs exceed the resources, and (10) being amazed at their own creativity, courage, and resourcefulness.

This is a brief introduction to one of the most common forms of off-campus ministries.[1] The crucial point to remember, however, is that this venture does not end with providing an army of social services. The long-term goal is to create an autonomous worshiping community.

Where Else?

Several parachurch organizations have created small worshiping communities that meet in a student's room in a college or university dormitory. At least three dozen charismatic renewal groups gather for worship every Saturday night in large hospitals.

The ministry with nursing home residents that begins with a party every month[2] can be expanded into a Bible study group that meets weekly. One of the most widespread off-campus ministries is the weekly Bible study and prayer group in a state or federal prison. Among the fastest-growing expressions of this concept is the English language congregation that organizes and staffs new off-campus congregations to serve newcomers from other lands. Another is the upper-middle class congregation that organizes an off-campus congregation for working-class residents who would never venture into that complicated building where nine out of ten worshipers adhere to a strict dress code from September through May.

One of the most interesting, and to some mature adults the most threatening, of these off-campus ministries originates in the white congregation with two identical and traditional worship services organized around the organ and classical music every Sunday morning. Instead of being content with the presence of a handful of seventeen to twenty-two year olds every week, a new venture is tried. One of the staff members, two or three adult volunteers (often high school teachers), and three dozen young adults in that age bracket create a planning committee. The goal is to design a meaningful worship experience organized around (1) a high level of participation by all worshipers, (2) peer leadership, (3) contemporary Christian music (which their parents may see as an oxymoron), (4) teaching sermons, and (5) fun.

Frequently these are held in a room in that congregation's meeting place on Saturday evening or concurrently with the late Sunday morning worship service. If, however, one goal is to reach beyond the social class restrictions of that congregation, an off-campus room is rented. This may be in the local high school or a vacant store downtown or in a shopping center.

Three Common Threads

This off-campus ministry with young adults also illustrates three threads that, while rarely discussed, are found in most off-campus ministries. The first is the importance of "our own place where we feel comfortable."[3] Many church leaders argue, "Instead of creating these off-campus ministries, we should invite those people to come here and worship with us and thus encourage the full integration of our congregation." A more precise version of that hope is "Instead of our going to their meeting place where they feel comfortable and we probably would feel uncomfortable, let us invite them to come to our meeting place where we are comfortable, even though that probably will make them feel uncomfortable, so we can achieve racial, cultural, and social class integration without surrendering anything we hold dear."

The normal attachment of human beings to a familiar place is a thread that runs through all of these ventures. The second best alternative is to choose a neutral site that is new to everyone in that gathering.

A second thread is what the scholars in the church growth movement have identified as the homogeneous unit principle. These off-campus ministries are organized on the principle that the participants have much in common. This may be social class, language, race, national origins, education, age, housing, income, employment, stage of their religious pilgrimage, earlier religious affiliation, preferences in music, family and marital status, or health. The greater the degree of homogeneity among the participants, the easier it is to create that new worshiping community.

The third thread, which has been lifted up earlier, is the value of focusing on the agenda of the people to be served, rather than seeking to impose someone else's agenda on the people to be served.

Twelve Lessons from Experience

What can be learned from the experiences of those who have pioneered off-campus ministries? In talking with the pioneers and in reflecting on their experiences, a dozen points are raised repeatedly.

First, a compelling vision of what could be is required to drive these ventures. Without a vision of a new tomorrow, we all are inclined to attempt to do yesterday over again.

Second, the initial focus must be on the needs and agenda of the people to be reached and served, not on the agenda of the servants. The first programs are designed in response to those needs.

Third, while it is true that an array of potential volunteers is out there waiting, they must be enlisted, inspired by the vision of what could be, trained, challenged, and supported. Perhaps the most widely neglected component of this strategy is the need for appropriate training for the volunteers.

Fourth, the closer the sponsoring congregation is to the high commitment end of that spectrum that runs from voluntary association to high commitment, the easier it will be to enlist volunteers.

Fifth, a continuing effort must be made to build and maintain the support of the sponsoring congregation for these off-campus ministries. A common tactic in this part of the larger strategy is to encourage adult classes, groups, choirs, and circles to adopt an off-campus ministry as their special outreach project.

Sixth, the administrative structure of these off-campus ministries usually is small in the early stages. That can be a big advantage in the beginning, but if it is not expanded, it will limit the potential growth.

Seventh, persistence in respecting, identifying, respecting, enlisting, respecting, training, and respecting indigenous leadership is essential.

Eighth, the governing board back at the sponsoring church must conceptualize its role as one of resourcing, supporting, encouraging, and applauding. If and when that governing board defines its role as a regulatory agency that has the authority to veto new ideas, creativity and initiative will suffer and potential indigenous leaders will flee.

Ninth, the prayer support of the people in the sponsoring church can be its number-one contribution.

Tenth, minimize financial subsidies. The goal is autonomy, not dependency!

Eleventh, one key to success is the continuity of the volunteer leadership. The higher the rate of turnover among the volunteers from the sponsoring church, the less likely the off-campus ministry will blossom. Ideally, at least one or two volunteers will marry the off-campus ministry they are related to and make that a long-term relationship.

Finally, the value of the continuing oversight of a minister (or director) of missions cannot be overstated. The absence of this person, who may be a volunteer, sharply increases the probability that these ventures will not enjoy a long life.

7.

WHAT ABOUT THE WOUNDED BIRDS?

"When a new mission field moves in, the church often moves out."
Harvey Kneisel.

In my district alone we have at least seven churches that probably should be closed," reflected a United Methodist District Superintendent.

"What are the criteria you use for coming to that conclusion?" questioned the Executive Presbyter of the Presbytery that covered approximately the same piece of territory.

"First, the largest of the seven averages fewer than three dozen people at worship on Sunday morning," promptly replied the superintendent. "None of them is even close to the size needed for a viable ministry. Second, every one of the seven has shrunk in size by at least 50 percent during the past twenty years. Third, all seven are subsidized, either directly or indirectly, by the annual conference. Fourth, if we didn't already have a church in that location, we would never start one there, and neither would you. All seven are relics from the days before people owned cars, and so they had to walk to church or go by horse and buggy."

"Well, why don't you go ahead and close them?" asked the executive presbyter.

"I guess I could," conceded the superintendent, "but that's a lot of work and takes more time than I have to spare. I would rather invest my time in more productive endeavors. I inherited all seven from my predecessor, and I guess I'll just bequeath them to my successor."

"Yeah, I guess benign neglect may be the best approach to these wounded birds. They still have too much life in them to roll over and die, but it's clear they'll never fly again," agreed the executive presbyter.

"I know exactly what you two are talking about," added a conference minister at this monthly luncheon of these three denominational officials. "I've never heard the term 'wounded birds' before, but that is a good analogy. One of our wounded birds is a nine-year-old new mission that peaked in size with over sixty at worship in its third year. About that time, the founding pastor left that new mission, his wife and family, and the professional ministry all in one day. The church is now served by his successor's successor and averages about thirty at worship. They owe our national board nearly a half million dollars on their mortgage and accumulated interest. They haven't made even an interest payment in three years. I don't think it ever will fly, but we don't have a simple procedure to put it out of its misery. If either one of you will give us $300,000, we'll sell you the land, that six-year-old building, and all of the members who want to join your denomination."

"Don't look at me," declared the executive presbyter. "We already have too many wounded birds. One of them is what was a promising new Anglo mission twenty years ago, but nearly all of the members have moved away and that neighborhood today is mostly Hispanic and African American. We've been looking for a black pastor to come in and redevelop it as an African American congregation, but thus far both of the two most promising candidates have turned us down. Currently the congregation, which is nearly all Anglo, is served by a retired Anglo pastor who is trying to hold the remnant together. He celebrated his seventieth birthday last month, so it is clear the future is not with him."

What Are the Alternatives?

Given the limited resources available to these three denominational leaders, what is their most promising course of action? One alternative is continued benign neglect. Provide assistance and counsel to the most promising congregations with the greatest potential for future ministry. Make that the top priority in allocating time, energy, and other resources. Let the wounded birds determine their own destiny.

A second is to bite the bullet and implement a strategy to close these churches that appear to have no future. In some denominations this is a more time-consuming and cumbersome procedure than in others.

Another course of action that had more supporters in the 1965–80 era than it appears to have today is to encourage two or three small struggling congregations to merge to form one viable church. This strategy offers greater promise when applied to disabled automobiles, trucks, or bicycles than it does with wounded birds.

A fourth alternative is to allocate the time necessary to encourage the lay leadership in these congregations to take the initiative and petition the denomination to close. While this often requires considerable time, patience, and the building of trust, it can eliminate the feeling of an adversarial relationship between that remnant and the denomination. It also reduces the level of guilt in the office of that regional judicatory.

A fifth possibility that is encouraged by a few traditions is to encourage the wounded birds to flock together to form a larger parish or some other form of cooperative arrangement. This is based on the assumption that shared weaknesses can become a source of mutual strength. This alternative still has considerable ideological support, but the historical record does not provide a foundation for optimism.

Where Are the Potential Resources?

A far more promising alternative is based on five assumptions. First, combining weakness with weakness by merging two wounded birds or by creating a larger parish can be a useful stop gap, but it rarely speaks to the heart of the problem. Second, the regional judicatories have limited resources, so that may not be the place to go for help. Third, the best approach is to begin with strength, not weaknesses. Fourth, and more important, the best prescription is not to seek to try to recreate yesterday, but rather to delineate a strategy for tomorrow. Finally, the best guideline is to minimize allocating resources to the dying and to direct those resources to giving birth to the new.

To be more specific, the most valuable resource in working with the wounded birds is not money or advice or sympathy or a desire to be helpful. The three most valuable resources to bring to these situations are (1) a vision of what could be, (2) hope, and (3) sensitivity and skill in identifying the needs of people who have never been a part of that worshiping community and in responding to those needs.[1]

What is the best place to look for those resources? One answer is in the large and strong congregation that has been receiving at least a hundred new members annually and that also displays a powerful future orientation. While not essential, it helps if this also is a high commitment congregation that persuasively projects high expectations of people.

What Next?

If all parties agree, and if the circumstances are appropriate, perhaps the best means of treating the wounded birds is to have a strong congregation adopt that ministry and enable it to fly again. In the corporate world, this often is described as a "take-over."

A working model of this strategy has been invented and implemented repeatedly by the First Baptist Church of Houston, Texas. Their experiences provide both examples of what can be done and lessons on how to do it.

The two key figures in this case study are Dr. John Bisagno, the outreach-oriented Senior Minister of this very large congregation which relocated to a new meeting place in 1976, and the Reverend Harvey Kneisel, who returned from the mission field in India in 1986. Kneisel subsequently became the Minister of Missions at First Baptist Church.

As the population of Houston grew in the years following World War II, it became increasingly pluralistic. As renters and members of ethnic minority groups moved into the inner sections of Houston, many of the whites moved out. Some moved to a community called Spring Branch just beyond the new inner loop highway. A new Baptist church was founded and gradually grew to over five hundred in Sunday school. The Westview Baptist Church was an outstanding success story of what a new mission could become. The congregation constructed an attractive set of buildings and prospered.

Two decades later, the white flight that had brought so many newcomers to Spring Branch was driving a new migration to new housing in new neighborhoods. As new multifamily housing developments were opened, and as the population of the community grew more diverse, the congregation at Westview Baptist Church grew older in years and smaller in numbers. Attendance dropped from over 500 to 50.

Similar scenarios were played out in scores of central-city churches all across the nation during the 1950–90 era. The next chapter usually represented one of three scenarios: (1) follow the members and relocate to a new neighborhood covered with new single-family homes or (2) close or (3) merge with another struggling church.

Fortunately the Westview Baptist Church was served by a wise pastor who saw a fourth alternative. He urged a merger with the huge mission-oriented First Baptist Church of Houston. The two congregations merged into one, and the title to the property was transferred to First Baptist Church.

About that same time the Reverend and Mrs. Harvey Kneisel returned from a tour of duty as church planting missionaries in India. Dr. John Bisagno invited Harvey Kneisel to plant a new church at the Westview site to serve a new constituency.

Mr. Kneisel believes in growth by multiplication, not by addition, so he surveyed the community to identify potential constituencies. He found the newcomers included 20,000 Asians, 30,000 blacks, 40,000 Hispanics, and 60,000 Anglos, most of them in the bottom third of the economic pyramid of Houston. Instead of planting one or two new congregations, he started five! Fifteen months later the combined attendance of these five new congregations was averaging 400 every Sunday.

As the years rolled by, other congregations responded to Dr. Bisagno's invitations to be adopted and nurtured by First Church. In early 1993, First Church was averaging 4,000 in Sunday school at their own site, and their off-campus congregations, including the newest off-campus missions, were averaging nearly two thousand. Several of these were new congregations that met in the buildings of congregations that had turned their property over to First Church. Others were new congregations meeting in apartments and other nontraditional locations. One was that mission in the Spring Brook apartments that had evolved into a congregation composed largely of children and teenagers. It is served by a bivocational minister who also teaches school. In early 1993, eight of the young men who had accepted Jesus Christ as Lord and Savior, while living in the Spring Brook apartments, were studying for the ministry at a

Baptist college, university, or seminary in Texas. Three of the young women were in college preparing to become missionaries. The constituency of these congregations includes Laotians, recent immigrants from Central America, low-income American-born Anglos, American-born blacks, Vietnamese, Africans, and Chinese. One of these began with the blending into one congregation of a black church with a white congregation. Another began with the blending of an aging Anglo constituency and a new group of younger Anglos.

All of the ministers serving these congregations are volunteers or bivocational pastors or indigenous leaders raised up out of that congregation. It also is a policy at First Baptist Church to encourage every adult department in the Sunday school to adopt one of these missions and to provide resources including volunteers, musicians, prayers, construction crews, outreach workers, and teachers.

What Is the Strategy?

From a strategic perspective the typical prescription for a wounded bird calls for the congregation to merge with a strong congregation. (For this discussion these will be called "sponsoring churches" or "missionary congregations.") The members of the wounded bird become members of this missionary church. Title to all real estate is transferred to the missionary church, often with the stipulation that it cannot be sold or otherwise disposed of for at least five years, unless it is turned over to a new congregation.

The missionary church usually brings six sets of resources to help the wounded bird.

1. A minister of missions who oversees and directs the process.

2. A cadre of trained, committed, future-oriented, and venturesome volunteers.

3. A strategy for defining a new constituency to be identified and served.

4. Skills in developing a ministry plan to reach and serve that new constituency.

5. Perhaps the most crucial of all, a conviction that the beginning point in implementing that strategy is to listen to and offer a sensitive and relevant response to the needs of the people who represent that new constituency. (At this point there is a substantial overlap between the strategies used in many other off-campus ministries described in chapter 6 and in working with wounded birds. The big difference is that the missionary church identified here begins with [a] the real estate owned by the wounded bird and [b] the remnant of that congregation.)

6. Since the central goal is to produce congregations that are capable of reaching and serving new constituencies and new generations of people, it is essential that the sponsor church possess a strong evangelistic spirit. If the potential sponsor church, regardless of size, is growing older and smaller due to an inability to respond effectively to the religious needs of new generations, it may be appropriate to identify it as a wounded bird. It would be inappropriate to ask it to function as a missionary church. This strong evangelistic spirit is an essential resource that the sponsor church brings to this strategy.

How Could This Work for You?

On December 31, 1990, The United Methodist Church included 7,702 congregations that reported an average worship attendance of twenty-five or less, including 1,530 reporting an average worship attendance of ten or less. The Southern Baptist Convention included nearly 4,000 congregations averaging twenty-five or less at worship. The American Baptist Churches reported 493 congregations averaging twenty-five or less at worship. In the Episcopal Church that total was 717. In the Christian Church (Disciples of Christ) the comparable figure was 317. In the United Church of Christ, 377 congregations reported an average worship attendance of twenty-five or fewer. A year later the Presbyterian Church (U.S.A.) reported 1,361 congregations in that size bracket, and the Evangelical Lutheran Church in America reported a total of 524. For the Assemblies of God, that figure was 1,390. For the Church of the Nazarene the comparable total was 621.

The total for these ten denominations was nearly 20,000—and that is based on the data submitted by the congregations that included a report of their average worship attendance. Another 7,000 congregations in these ten denominations did not report their worship attendance.

What will the future bring to these congregations? Dissolution? Merger? Sharp numerical growth? Continued numerical decline? Stability? Joining a larger parish?

An attractive alternative for at least 5,000 or 6,000 of these small churches could be to accept their identity as wounded birds, ask a larger, strong, and outreach-oriented congregation to take them over, and ask that missionary church to help them (a) define a new constituency and (b) formulate a ministry plan to reach that new constituency. With some small-town congregations, one possibility would be to redefine their role into that of a regional church with the assistance of another regional missionary church. With many open-country and central-city congregations, it could be to help pioneer a new role for the missionary church as a multisite parish. (See chapter 8.)

Another flock of wounded birds consists of those new missions of five to twelve years ago that peaked in size with a hundred or less at worship and have been shrinking in size for the past several years.

What is the future for those 65,000 or 70,000 Protestant congregations that average between 26 and 50 at worship? That list includes 2,900 congregations affiliated with the Assemblies of God, nearly a thousand American Baptist congregations, more than a thousand Episcopal parishes and missions, 1,500 Evangelical Lutheran parishes, a thousand in the Presbyterian Church (U.S.A.), more than 7,600 Southern Baptist congregations, and over 9,000 United Methodist churches. It would be poor stewardship to close them. Why abandon what in many cases is valuable real estate for missional purposes? Most cannot afford a full-time resident pastor. Yoking them with one or two other congregations to share one minister has not been an outstanding success. Merging them with another congregation often fulfills the generalization that in mergers 30 plus 40 is more likely to equal 35 or 40 or 50, not 70.[2]

One alternative is to encourage them to be served by a bivocational pastor. That alternative has produced many more successes than failures.

The issue here is not the record of bivocational pastors. The issue is what is the most effective support system for bivocational ministers? One widely followed alternative has been to encourage or require bivocational ministers to identify with the other ministers in that denomination in general and in the regional judicatory in particular. A second has been to relate to the national home missions agency of that denomination.

From this observer's perspective the most promising alternative is for bivocational ministers to look to a large, supportive, nurturing, and outreach-oriented congregation with substantial discretionary resources as their primary reference point. Idcally it is the one they joined several years earlier. Each missionary congregation can enlist, train, and oversee three to fifteen or more bivocational pastors from among their members. Each bivocational pastor can have his or her (or their, since many of these are married couples) individual support system in an adult Sunday school class or a Tuesday evening Bible study group or a Saturday morning gathering of these bivocational ministers. An excellent model of this last alternative is the four o'clock Sunday afternoon gathering at the First Baptist Church of Arlington, Texas. With the dynamic leadership of Tillie Burgin, this becomes an exciting time of sharing, worship, singing, Bible study, reflection, celebration, and inspiration.

These sponsor or missionary congregations also can offer the classroom as well as the practical training sought by bivocational pastors. The experienced bivocational ministers can serve as models and mentors for the most recent volunteers to this growing army.

What about those 60,000 Protestant congregations that average between fifty and eighty at worship? They are too large to close, too small to attract, challenge, afford, and keep a full-time, seminary-trained, and competent pastor, too valuable to merge, too independent to "go on the dole" of a perpetual denominational subsidy, and too numerous to ignore. Furthermore, frequently the work load is too large for the typical bivocational pastor with a full-time secular job.

One of the most attractive alternatives is to create a team of three bivocational pastors who will provide the needed ministerial leadership. Sometimes all three are longtime friends who come out of the same adult Sunday school class in that missionary church. Occasionally the team consists of one member from the congregation to be served plus two from that sponsor church.

More than 7,500 of the congregations in this size bracket carry a United Methodist identification, another 7,000 are Southern Baptists, more than 2,300 are Assemblies of God, well over a thousand are Episcopal, another thousand are Church of the Nazarene, more than a thousand are in the United Church of Christ, nearly two thousand carry the label of the Evangelical Lutheran Church in America, more than a thousand are in the Lutheran Church-Missouri Synod, nearly two thousand are Presbyterian Church (U.S.A.), and over a thousand are American Baptist.

Most of them could be candidates for this model of ministry. While there continues to be a significant amount of social status attached to "having our own full-time pastor who is a seminary graduate," that alternative carries many disadvantages. With the price of seminary graduates rising faster than people's incomes, more and more small- to middle-sized congregations are being priced out of the ministerial marketplace. The tenure tends to be short for recent seminary graduates who do go to serve full-time in a congregation averaging under one hundred at worship. The most competent and productive often are soon called to serve a larger and "more challenging" congregation. In recent years a large proportion of seminary graduates who go to this size congregation for their first pastorate decide within a decade to leave the parish ministry. Is that a productive pattern?

The bivocational team concept (a) enables each of the three to perfect a specialty in ministry; (b) provides a sense of continuity—when one member of that team departs and is replaced, the other two socialize that newcomer into "how we do ministry here," for the continuity is in the team, not in one individual; (c) taps that growing number of competent, skilled, dedicated, and eager members in that large missionary church who feel a call to do more than serve on one more committee; (d) offers that small church the equivalent in varied skills of a staff team, but at far less than the compensation required for one resident pastor; (e) brings to that small congregation a ministerial team that has experienced the fact that a congregation can rise beyond survival goals and put outreach at the top of the local agenda; (f) frees up financial resources for new forms of ministry; and (g) minimizes the temptation in smaller congregations to "let the minister do it" and thus create an excessive dependency on paid help. (It is not unusual for all three members of that bivocational team to live five to thirty or more miles from the meeting place of the congregation they serve. That can be an asset in minimizing dependency.)

That large church can spare three of its best leaders without seriously depleting its roster of talent; it can serve as a support group for that team; it can supply a replacement who will be a compatible match when one member of that team departs; it can offer challenging training experiences for that team that go beyond "how to maintain the institution"; it can help to resource new ministries, events, and experiences for people in that smaller congregation that are beyond the competence of the regional judicatory to provide; it can be a resource for strategic planning; and it can provide emergency substitutes on very short notice if one member of the team must be absent on very short notice. This can be a "win-win" model for these small- to middle-sized congregations as well as for that bivocational team and the sponsoring church. (The bivocational team of three to five specialists may be the best alternative for staffing congregations that average 80 to 125 at worship. In today's world it is not unusual for one or more members of these bivocational teams to be seminary graduates.)

Perhaps the most widely analyzed flock of wounded birds includes those Anglo congregations that were created to serve an all-Anglo neighborhood. As the white population moved out and was replaced by, to use Harvey Kneisel's phrase, a new mission field moving in, one option was for that white congregation to relocate. A better alternative may be to affiliate with a missionary church and turn the title to the real estate over to that missionary congregation.

Six Key Lessons

In addition to what has been learned by other experiences in off-campus ministries that are described in the previous chapter, six additional lessons come out of these experiences with wounded birds.

First, instead of seeing that wounded bird as a problem or liability, it should be perceived as an asset.

Second, and this goes back to the central theme of this book, in an era of (a) decentralization, (b) shrinking denominational resources, and (c) escalating demands, the most effective means of expanding resources is to challenge congregations in general, and lay volunteers in particular, to accept new outreach responsibilities.

Third, that missionary church can bring many assets to help restore the wounded birds to health. Number one is the conviction that healthy congregations are organized around mission, evangelism, proclamation, the teaching ministry, and responding to the religious needs of people, not around institutional survival goals. Number two is assistance in identifying new audiences. Number three is the strong visionary future orientation brought by those volunteers. Number four is fresh leadership. Number five is the absence of a desire to perpetuate local traditions. Number six is the commitment to mission and evangelism of those volunteers, and number seven may be other resources, such as skilled labor to renovate the physical facilities, teachers, musicians, money, or educational resources.

Fourth, the goal is not to enable that wounded bird to fly back into yesterday, but rather to help it become a resource for a new tomorrow. A useful parallel is the mythical story of the Egyptian phoenix bird that was resurrected from the ashes to start a new life. The concept of a resurrection is consistent with the Christian faith!

Fifth, this strategy is designed to bring strength, not weakness, to the wounded birds.

Sixth, either the pastor of the missionary church must accept the role as minister of missions, or at least a part-time minister of missions should be added to the staff of the missionary church.

Finally, the strategy cannot focus on the dream of recreating yesterday. It must focus on identifying a new constituency and/or a new role for that wounded bird.

Yes, that wounded bird can fly again, but it won't be the same old bird, and it may fly higher and farther, as well as in a new direction.

8.

THE MULTISITE OPTION

My guess is perhaps 30 percent of our people are opposed to relocation, at least 40 percent recognize that our chances for continued growth are severely limited in this building at this location, and close to 30 percent haven't made up their minds," observed a veteran leader of this eighty-nine-year-old congregation. During the past seven years, the average worship attendance jumped from 340 to nearly 600. Sunday school attendance nearly doubled as this downtown church found itself growing younger and larger since the arrival of a new senior minister seven years earlier.

"That's not quite the way I see it," commented the oldest member of the Long Range Planning Committee. "I think we have four groups here. The most numerous, but far from a majority, are those who want to relocate. The second largest group, and I consider myself to be in this camp, is composed of those who feel this church is now as large as any church should be. We favor planting a new mission as one way to relieve the pressure. A third group has yet to take a stand. The smallest group is opposed to relocation, but they don't have a positive course of action to offer."

"It seems to me we have three choices," summarized another volunteer leader. "We can plateau in size at this location, we can relocate, or we can send out a nucleus of a hundred or so members to plant a new mission and get us down to the size this building will accommodate."

Which of those three choices appears to you to be the most attractive?

The Both-And Alternative

Before answering that question, it may be wise to look at another alternative that is becoming increasingly popular. When the members are sharply divided between those who argue, "Let's relocate to a new and larger site and construct a new and modern building," and those who contend, "Let's continue at this site in this historic building," the compromise answer is "Yes."

To be more specific, this course of action means continuing to offer a full schedule of programming at the old site while concurrently offering a duplicate schedule in a new building in a new location. This response combines continuing the traditional package of ministries, including the corporate worship of God and part of the teaching ministry on the old campus, and adding new events, experiences, services, and classes at a new "off-campus" location. This can be an effective means of pioneering the new without abandoning the old.

Observers of this approach to ministry usually ask five sets of questions that now can be answered from experience.

How Long?

The least significant of these questions is asked most often: "How long will we continue with two meeting places?" The most widely practiced answer is for five to ten years. The multisite or dual campus arrangement is in fact often a short-term strategy. The congregation continues with two meeting places until

(a) sufficient facilities have been constructed at the new location to house the total ministry, and/or (b) the skeptics who opposed the relocation have had adequate time to experience the benefits and advantages of the new facilities and to persuade themselves that relocation is the best course of action, and/or (c) a purchaser is found for the old site, and/or (d) four or five funerals have been conducted for the last-ditch opponents of relocation.

A better answer is "We don't know." That response is based on the assumption that the most valuable legacy today's leaders can offer the next generation is the optimum range of attractive choices. In other words, this answer trusts the next generation of leaders to make a wise decision within the context of tomorrow's world.

A third and increasingly common response is "This is the first step toward becoming a church that serves people from two or three different locations. While future leaders may revise the plans, we expect this will continue for many decades as a multisite church."

A radically different response is "Until sufficient people with adequate resources gather at the new site for it to become a separate and self-governing congregation." In other words, this can be one strategy for "mothering" strong new missions. Closing out the old site was never on the list of alternatives in this strategy.

Another answer to that "how long" question is "When the recently arrived pastor(s) conclude that the cost of maintaining this dual campus arrangement in terms of time and energy exceeds the benefits."

A parallel is the church that for many years has scheduled three worship services every Sunday morning. The new pastor arrives and soon announces, "This schedule is too divisive; it asks too much of the staff, of our adult choirs, and of our ushers, and it is undermining our Sunday school." The board agrees to cut back to two worship services on Sunday morning.

What Is Your Denominational Policy?

From a denominational perspective, two important policy questions deserve attention. First, does your denomination in general, and your regional judicatory officials in particular, encourage congregations to implement this strategy? When a large and growing congregation purchases twenty or thirty or seventy or ninety acres as the site for its second meeting place, this may threaten congregations meeting in a building within five miles of that site. Is your denominational strategy based on the assumption that people should and will go to neighborhood churches? Does your strategy assume that people in the year 2025 will prefer small neighborhood congregations? Or will they prefer large regional churches?

Second, is your regional judicatory prepared to accept the role of challenging existing congregations to initiate off-campus ministries much as those described in the previous two chapters? If yes, can that range of challenges be expanded to include challenging congregations to consider the multisite option?

If the answer to both of these policy questions is negative, that may help to explain why this option is more common among (a) independent congregations and (b) denominations following a congregational polity.

Why?

At least a dozen reasons have been offered to explain the benefits of the multisite strategy. Six stand out repeatedly. One is to break the stalemate between remaining at the old site and relocation. Those who oppose abandoning a sacred site that houses so many meaningful memories do not have to yield. Those who want new facilities on a larger site at a more strategic location also can have their way. Both groups are winners. There are no losers.

For those with a particular set of values, the key reason for the multisite option is that it offers the possibility of reaching and serving a larger and more diverse group of people than could be achieved by concentrating all resources at only one place. Some will be attracted by the combination of location, people, schedule, facilities, and program at one site, while others will prefer what is offered at the other site. The multisite option is especially attractive to those interested in reaching larger numbers of people. A fringe benefit can be growth with a minimum degree of crowding, complexity, and anonymity.

This is one means of making a fresh start in identifying a new constituency and designing a new package of ministries to reach and serve that new constituency who will not come to the present site.

A third obvious reason is that the larger membership can provide the financial resources needed to purchase the land and construct the new buildings. If a couple of hundred members were left to do this on their own, it would take far longer to mobilize the necessary financial resources.

Far more important than money, however, is that the dual campus or multisite option retains the advantages of a large and competent staff, a large cadre of volunteer leaders, and the institutional strength of a big church for implementing the total ministry. Dividing into two congregations undermines that institutional strength.

A fifth reason can be summarized by the word *choice*. By continuing to function as one congregation with one governing board, one staff, one treasury, and one total program, the multisite church can offer people a broader range of choices than either could if the decision had been made to divide and become two separate churches.

A sixth reason is illustrated by the Mount Paran Church of God on Atlanta's west side. This Pentecostal congregation outgrew its new building on an attractive site at an excellent location. When it could not expand its physical facilities because of zoning restrictions, it became a multisite congregation. It quickly grew into one congregation with five widely scattered meeting places.

How Do They Do It?

The most complex of these five often-asked questions is directed at the *how.* Experience suggests several guidelines for those who want to utilize the multisite option. The most obvious is that this means one governing board, one set of administrative committees, one budget, one treasury, one staff, one senior minister, and one definition of purpose and role. The organizational structure may include a variety of program committees and two sets of trustees, each with one piece of property to maintain.

The most subtle, and perhaps the most critical, is hidden under the term "one staff." This means one senior minister with one program staff. It also means the primary loyalty of each member is to the concept and the rest of the program staff, not to a particular place. That distinction disqualifies all potential staff members who prefer to build their own empire in isolation from the rest of the program.

(At least a few readers will contend that another alternative is to discard the hierarchical concept that includes a senior minister and rely on a staff team. That may be a possibility, but it is difficult to find large Protestant congregations today led by an egalitarian staff team rather than by a senior minister. It is even more difficult to find examples of large multisite churches led by an egalitarian staff team. The "team" concept may be the wave of the future, but that model has yet to be perfected.)

If the arrangement includes two sites, it usually means the senior minister will preach at both places on at least thirty-five Sunday mornings every year. If it includes three sites, the senior minister typically will preach at two of the three (or three out of the three) sites on at least thirty-five or forty weekends every year and at each place at least twenty-six weekends annually.

The central component in helping people conceptualize this as one congregation is that "At least half the Sundays every year, my senior minister is in the pulpit where I worship."

At this point it should be noted that another component of that larger strategy of reaching and serving more people may be to schedule weekly Saturday evening worship experiences at one or both locations.

It is impossible to overemphasize the importance of the unreserved commitment of the senior pastor and the program staff if this option is to continue indefinitely. The arrival of a new senior minister who cannot conceptualize the values of this arrangement is the most effective way to terminate it.

Another critical component of this option is that neither site be perceived as "second-class." This need is one reason why the senior minister must preach at both sites. This decision requires both worship and Sunday school every Sunday at both places. It usually means that the location of the annual congregational meeting rotates from one site to another. It often means the governing board rotates the place of its monthly meeting. It means new members will be received at both sites and that baptisms and Holy Communion will be celebrated at both places.

In middle-sized arrangements, the early Sunday morning service will be scheduled for one site and the late service for the other place. As soon as the numbers are sufficient to encourage it, however, the schedule will include two worship services at each site—often with Sunday school between the two services. This often means that one minister preaches the early-service sermon at one site and the second-service sermon at the other, while a colleague follows the reverse schedule.

In larger congregations, the typical Sunday morning schedule calls for two or three worship services at each place in addition to a full Sunday school. The vacation Bible school, scheduled for early in the summer, will be held at one site and the one scheduled for late summer will be held at the other site. Each campus continues with the full range of basic programming.[1]

How Many?

How many different sites can serve as ministry centers under the umbrella of one congregation? One answer is that no one knows. A second is well over a hundred. In implementing the Key Church Strategy described in chapter 5, the First Baptist Church of Arlington, with the remarkable leadership of Tillie Burgin, staffs well over a hundred off-campus ministries.

For most congregations, however, the answer "Two or three" will be most reassuring. The best answer, however, is "It all depends." The number should be consistent with the local goals and resources.

If the central goal is to offer a full-scale, seven-day-a-week program at each location with an average worship attendance of at least three hundred at each site, the best answer probably is two or three. Putting four or more full-service congregations under one administrative umbrella usually will require allocating more resources for management than can be justified by the results.

If the senior minister is determined to maintain a frequent and highly visible presence at each campus, the answer is probably two.

If, however, the chief motivating force is evangelism and missions, if this is a high-commitment congregation, and if the staff includes a competent and enthusiastic full-time minister of missions, a reasonable goal is one off-campus center for ministry for every one hundred people at worship in the average weekday. (Note: It may be wise to avoid use of the term *satellite*. That has led those worshiping at the off-campus site to view themselves as second class. *Ministry center* or *chapel* may be less controversial words. Probably the best is the two-site congregation that refers to "The North Campus" or "The West Campus" or "First Church East" and "First Church South.")

If the goal is to use this concept as a strategy for launching what is expected will become self-governing, self-expressing, self-financing, and self-propagating new congregations, a reasonable goal would be one new off-campus congregation every two or three years.

If the congregation has only one pastor on the staff and averages fewer than two hundred at worship, the best answer to that "how many" question probably is one or none. The exception would be if this is seen as the first stage of a long-term process for the relocation of the meeting place.

If the pastor or senior minister expects to resign or retire within the next three years, the best answer probably is zero. Do not pass to a successor your self-designed monument to your own ministry.

An Easier Alternative

Lest anyone be misled by the apparent attractiveness of this model of ministry, it is not an easy-to-implement option! The easiest alternative consists of an attractive and comfortable two-part strategy. The first part is to watch passively as the congregation grows older in the age of the members and smaller in numbers. The second component of this passive strategy is to watch other congregations, including new missions, offer the ministries and program necessary to reach new generations of people. As long as some other church is reaching and serving those younger generations, why should we worry? We enjoy our comfortable, warm, intimate, and caring fellowship, so why change?

Between the strategy of growing older and smaller and the multisite option lies a third alternative, which also often is easier to implement than the multisite option. That is the complete relocation of the meeting place.[2] While that creates a core of unhappy members, it is less complicated and cleaner than the multisite option.

Variations on the Basic Concept

The seven most highly visible expressions of the multisite option are (a) the downtown church with the satellite that is little more than a preaching point, not a seven-day-a-week ministry center; (b) the urban church with two or three or four off-campus meeting places; (c) the use of this option as one step in an extended relocation process; (d) the predominantly black central-city congregation and the predominantly Anglo suburban congregation; (e) as a product of the Key Church Strategy described in chapter 5; (f) as an expression of the large congregation caring for wounded birds, described in chapter 7; and (g) as a practical strategy for "mothering" new missions.

What probably will turn out to be the most widely followed use of the concept, however, began to appear in rural America in the 1950s. The typical arrangement calls for an administrative merger of one or two or three small open-country churches with a larger congregation in town. The desired result is one governing board, one budget, one treasury, one staff, three Sunday schools, three sets of trustees, three meeting places, and three or four or five worship services on Sunday morning. In a typical arrangement, the senior minister preaches in one of the two small congregations on alternate Sundays as well as in the town church on Sunday morning, while the associate (who may be a licensed but not ordained preacher) preaches at the early service in town and alternates between the two small churches. (One of the two small congregations has worship followed by Sunday school, while the other has Sunday school followed by worship.)

The details of the schedule obviously must reflect the local scene in terms of location in the time zone, distance between buildings, variables in staffing, and seasonal differences in attendance.

Is the multisite alternative an option your church should explore? It may help in answering that question to review three very different experiences with this model of ministry.

The Perimeter Experience

One of the most creative ventures in a new model for the parish ministry dates back to the summer of 1977, when Randy Pope was called by the Presbyterian Church in America to plant a new mission on the north side of Atlanta. The vision called for planting a series of additional new churches in that suburban area. The design called for one congregation, one senior minister, one budget, one treasury, and several meeting places. By 1980 the second congregation was launched with Pope preaching every Sunday morning at both sites. Soon a third and a fourth congregation were planted, and the dream became reality.

By 1989 this pioneering new ministry included five congregations meeting in five locations with a monthly worship experience on Sunday evening in a hotel ballroom with close to 1,600 people in attendance from all five Perimeter congregations.

Success brought its problems, as it always does. The managerial burden on Randy Pope grew heavier and began to crowd out ministry. From day one the goal had been ministry, not institution building. It became apparent that this arrangement carried four price tags. First, it was becoming increasingly difficult to plant additional new churches—and that had been a primary goal of the dream. Second, the leaders concluded that the management responsibilities were making it increasingly difficult for Perimeter Church to fulfill its role as a resource to other congregations. Third, Randy Pope needed to spend more time back at the ranch at Perimeter Church. Finally, the elders concluded that the most creative and productive role for Perimeter Church to the other congregations would be to influence, rather than direct, what happened in the other congregations in the Perimeter Family of Churches.

Thus in 1990 the leaders made the decision, reluctantly but amicably, to dissolve the original design and replace it with an association of completely self-governing, self-financing, and self-propagating congregations.

Two years later one of the leaders from the Perimeter Church described it as "the same feeling one would have if all four of your children left home on the same day." The time had come for each one to go its own way, but the parents of this venture experienced a mixture of loving concern, regret, and rejoicing as that tightly knit family dispersed.

What happened next?

A sixth congregation was planted in Athens, Georgia, and in early 1993 plans were being finalized to plant a seventh in Buckhead and an eighth in Atlanta. Perimeter Church, the original congregation, was receiving 300 new members annually and had grown to an average worship attendance of 1,400 by the end of 1992. In early 1992 a ninety-acre relocation site had been purchased four miles to the north. That ministry had outgrown the 20-acre parcel on Spalding Road.

This 1,300-member congregation also has accepted a role as a teaching church, offering the twice-a-year "Perimeter Weekend" to pastors and congregational leaders who want to come and learn from this congregation's experiences.

What happened to that original dream of ringing the perimeter of Norcross with several campuses of what would continue as one congregation with one staff and one governing board?

The response was larger than the dream. The new and more comprehensive dream called for the creation of that new 501(c)3 corporation in 1990 called Perimeter Ministries International (PMI). This association of autonomous congregations is governed by a board consisting of elders from each of the participating congregations. It is an outreach mission of these churches with a three-person staff, and it exists to accomplish these three primary objectives:

1. To plant and nurture healthy churches reaching a variety of socioeconomic and ethnic groups, both here and abroad;

2. To unite the resources of each member church to make an impact on our culture by ministering to the under-resourced people of Atlanta and targeting groups that shape the social, economic, political, and economic structures of our society; and
3. To resource our existing churches with materials, ideas, and training for effective ministry.

An Ohio Model

While still in its early stages, the experiences of First Community Church in suburban Columbus, Ohio, illustrate several important lessons for those contemplating the multisite option. As was pointed out earlier, the easiest-to-implement strategy is to drift quietly and passively while watching the congregation grow older and smaller. A more difficult alternative is to sell the old meeting place and construct new facilities on a new site. The most difficult of these three alternatives is the multisite option.

Over the years, First Community Church (FCC) has earned a reputation as a remarkably innovative congregation. It is one of the most widely studied churches in American Protestantism and has been served by several exceptionally creative pastors. By the mid-1980s, this diverse, inclusive, and creative congregation had accumulated many assets, including a program staff of ten professionals; a thirteen-hundred-acre campground; a retirement community with over four hundred residents; a beautiful sanctuary; a payroll of forty full-time employees; a sophisticated network-quality television studio and a huge television audience; an earned reputation as a teaching church; a big missions program; hundreds of creative members, many with very high expectations of their church; an average attendance of approximately a thousand at Sunday morning worship; and a host of rich memories from the past.

The liabilities included aging buildings on an inadequate site, church-owned off-street parking for only eighty-five vehicles, the absence of a large fellowship hall, severely limited facilities for adult Christian education, a third-rate nursery, second-rate restrooms, fourth-rate facilities for youth programming, and at least a few neighbors who objected to churchgoers who parked in the streets or blocked their driveways.

Forty years earlier, one of America's famous ministers, Roy Burkhart, whose twenty-six-year tenure as senior minister at FCC ended in 1958, had proposed relocation, and a twenty-acre relocation site had been purchased. Nothing happened. His successor, Otis Maxfield, also pushed for relocation, but it did not happen, and eventually that twenty-acre site was sold. (Three of the most frequently articulated cries of frustration in congregational circles are [1] "We used to own it and we sold it"; [2] "We could have bought it for a song, and today the present owners want a million dollars for it"; and [3] "We refused to buy it when it was available; now it is not available at any price.")

A Long Range Planning Committee was appointed in 1986, and, after two years of work, recommended relocation. An option was secured on an eighteen-acre site five miles northwest of the current meeting place. The vote was taken on Sunday, May 10, 1989. A total of 1,989 members voted. To the surprise and chagrin of many of the leaders and the staff, 1,109 voted against relocation. The constitution of FCC required a congregational vote, and each vote carried the same weight, whether cast by an active leader or a member who had rarely attended during the past two decades.[3]

This is one of the crucial lessons in any strategy for change. Any system of decision making that gives the same weight to the vote of the passive observer that is given to the vote of the active leader is "loaded" against change.[4] As will be illustrated by subsequent events in this account, a more productive strategy is to count the support of those willing to invest their time, energy, creativity, and money on a new tomorrow. That is the first lesson from the Ohio experience.

The second lesson is that proposals for radical change often must be presented several times before they are implemented.

Twice earlier, FCC had before it a proposal to relocate. The central point to remember is that failure to implement or rejection of a proposal for radical change should not be interpreted as defeat. All it really means is "Not yet."

Both lessons were learned and included in the next stage. The new plan, "By Faith . . . Together!" was presented in early 1990. It was designed around a "win-win" theme and included two major proposals. One was to renovate the old plant. The second was to create a "Center for Extended Ministry" at the new site. Instead of seeking 1,200 positive votes, the goal of the previous year, the new goal was seven million yes votes. Each vote cost a dollar, everyone could vote as often as they wanted, *and* the voters could designate whether that vote was "For" the new center or "For" the renovation of the old historic building. This system of voting did not include the option of casting "Against" votes.

Slightly over two million votes were cast for remodeling the old facilities and another four million for launching the Center for Extended Ministry. That vote illustrates a third lesson from the Ohio experience. The love for that old sacred place, the hope to perpetuate the past, and the preference for modest changes can be powerful motivating forces! At FCC it produced two million votes.

The celebration of the completion of the remodeling program was held in the fall of 1991. Concurrently, the construction of the facilities at the Center was being completed. These included a large multipurpose room that can seat 400 to 600 for worship (and create the impression it is "full" when only 300 chairs are filled, but the 400 additional chairs held in reserve can be used to accommodate a larger crowd), and also can be used for concerts, dinners, and other large-crowd events. The capacity for children's ministries was doubled by building facilities for a new Child Care Center at the north site while remodeling the Preschool at the south site. A youth lounge, offices, restrooms, and meeting rooms also were included in the building program at the Center at the north site.

The Center officially opened on December 8, 1991. In 1992 worship attendance at the north site averaged 400 with only the one service at nine o'clock Sunday morning followed by Sunday school classes and seminars at 10:15 A.M That worship experience is designed for younger adults and includes drama, contemporary Christian music, and less formal worship than at the south site.

At the south site a liturgical Holy Communion service at 8:30 Sunday morning replaced the former nine o'clock service, and the traditional eleven o'clock service was maintained. The senior minister preached early at the Center and at eleven o'clock at the old site.

Despite the sudden resignation of the Senior Minister for personal reasons in mid-1992, worship attendance in 1992 was up nearly 9 percent from the 1991 average. Summer worship attendance showed a 55 percent increase! The Easter 1992 worship attendance was the highest since 1968, and the combined attendance for Easter 1993 was 2,874.

A fourth lesson from First Community Church, and one of the central arguments for the multisite option, is that it can create a "win-win" decision. The winners included those who had strong ties to the old familiar place and wanted only to remodel those facilities. Likewise, the winners included those who wanted to reach new generations of younger families, to expand the total ministry and program, to expand the range of choices, and to upgrade the quality of the meeting place.

A fifth lesson is that only in the existence of a widely perceived crisis is it easy to move fast. Nearly forty years elapsed between the time when "Burkie" (Dr. Roy Burkhart) first proposed relocation and the opening of the Center on a different site.

Sixth, nostalgia, the past, feelings, and emotion often are more influential motivators than logic, reason, and a concern for the future in responding to proposals for change.

Seventh, the single most effective method of reaching new generations is to invite them to help pioneer new ministries at a new site in a new building that is not filled with traditions and precedents.

An eighth lesson, mentioned above, is still being debated at First Community Church. This is the power of the name. Why not call the old site the "Center" and the new north property the "Satellite"? One reason is that each of those names carries a lot of baggage. A common solution is to identify one as the South Campus and the other as the North Campus. Both are neutral terms. No one wants to be described as second class. Likewise, no one wants to have the other group identified as the "first team" or the "first class" site.

Another positive lesson from the FCC experience is the importance of program staff rotating through both facilities. Each program staff member needs to have high visibility at both locations. Some will have their offices at the new site, and some will be housed at the old site, but all need to be visible at both locations. Closely related to that is scheduling programming in a manner that encourages every member to see each site as a familiar place and as "my church home."

Perhaps the most subtle lesson that comes out of the multisite experiences is the difficulties that long-established program committees encounter in creating new approaches to ministry, worship, music, and programming at the new site. Standing committees tend to be heavily influenced by precedent, tradition, boundaries, and yesterday.[5] One solution is to create ad hoc task forces and delegate to them the responsibility for designing new ministries. A common one is to have two choir directors or two ministers of music. One is to organize and implement a ministry of music at the old site. The other is responsible for organizing and directing a new ministry of music designed to reach and include a new constituency at the new site.

When one of the primary reasons for choosing the multisite option is to reach a new constituency, it is essential that the new ministries and new programs not be seen as carbon copies or extensions of what has been offered at the old site.

One of the advantages of the FCC experience is that the new north site is across the river and in a different public school district. By having two youth ministers (plus one of the veteran ministers on the staff) at the north site, plus new and better facilities, this made it comparatively easy to initiate new ministries with teenagers. The "postgame" parties on Friday or Saturday evening have attracted over a hundred teenagers, many of whom had never been to FCC before. The Saturday "3 on 3" basketball tournament and the coed volleyball league also provided attractive entry points in reaching new constituencies of teenagers.

One of the most crucial lessons also is illustrated by the FCC experience. Who will be the key staff person based at the new site? The wrong answer is a minister who will seek to build a personal constituency as one step in creating a separate empire.

The right answer, which was what happened at FCC, is to choose a long-tenured, highly competent, personable, and respected staff member who can relate to a broad range of people and who will, by both word and deed, repeatedly reinforce the concept that this is *one* congregation with *one* staff that meets at two different sites. The only more important ingredient in implementing the multisite option is to have a senior minister who is unreservedly committed to this approach to ministry! The minister based at the new site also must earn the complete trust of that senior minister. It helps if each of these two ministers preaches at both locations at least thirty-five or forty times a year.

One of the more difficult issues that usually surfaces when this option is implemented is governance. In the vast majority of American Protestant congregations, the governing board is tempted to accept the responsibility for telling others what they cannot do. Implementation of the multisite option requires that the one governing board redefine its role.

Instead of functioning as a permission-giving and permission-withholding board, the multisite option calls for the church council to combine four major responsibilities: (1) serving as a permanent futures or long-range planning committee; (2) challenging the staff, standing committees, task forces, and ad hoc committees to create new ministries to reach and serve new constituencies; (3) making policy decisions on priorities in the allocation of scarce resources; and (4) acting as a support group for the staff. This role requires the capability to trust committees to carry out their responsibilities.

One of the most difficult facets of this model is that the multisite option requires people to replace the word *competition* in their thinking about ministry with the word *complement*. One example of this can be seen when a regional judicatory announces plans to plant a new mission that eventually will meet in a building to be constructed near the intersection of X Boulevard and Y Avenue. Leaders in congregations meeting in buildings within three miles of that intersection often feel threatened by that announcement. They fear competition. Usually what happens is not what was feared. First, on the typical weekend, a majority of the residents living within five miles of that intersection continue not going to church anywhere. Second, that new mission complements the role of existing congregations. It reaches a slice of the population largely not reached by those other churches. Third, if that new mission does experience rapid numerical growth, that motivates at least a couple of the nearby churches to take the steps necessary to improve their ministry in order "to keep up with the competition."

A parallel pattern often appears when the multisite option is implemented. One fear is "This will split our church." Another is "We must not compete against ourselves, so we will never schedule competing worship experiences at the same hour, except maybe on Easter Sunday." A third fear is "We don't want to give the impression that the old place is for the old people and the new site is for younger families."

One response to those fears is "Nonsense."

A second response is that the foundation of Christianity is faith, not fear.

A better response is to see the ministries at these two locations complementing each other.

The best response is "The issue is not avoiding competition by cutting back on the schedule. The reason we chose the multisite option is to reach more people with the gospel of Jesus Christ. We can best do that with full scale programming and a full schedule at both locations."

The two big exceptions to that are (1) the annual congregational meeting will be held on the East Campus in even-numbered years and the West Campus in odd-numbered years and (2) certain anniversary celebrations can be held only at one site because of space or schedule limitations at the other.

Finally, the First Community Church experience will offer American Protestantism an important lesson. What happens when that creative senior minister departs seven or eight months after the first building program has been completed at the second site and new ministries are still in their formative stages? One answer to that question will be written in central Ohio in the mid-1990s.

A Texas Model

While it is still too early to evaluate it, what may turn out to be an exceptionally relevant model is being pioneered by the First United Methodist Church of Houston. This historic downtown church with nearly 14,000 members purchased a 27.4 acre site eight miles to the west in 1992.

A "preview" worship service was scheduled in December with an attendance of 450. Regular Sunday morning worship was scheduled beginning the second Sunday in January 1993. The Senior Minister, Dr. William Hinson, preaches every week at nine o'clock, which is designed as a Wesleyan contemporary worship experience. During the first several weeks it averaged over 400 in attendance. The thirty-three-year-old associate minister is the preacher at the eleven o'clock service, which was averaging 250 to 300 in attendance in early 1993. The target audience for this hour is illustrated by this preacher's theme for Lent, "A Thirty-Something Savior." This service also includes drama, contemporary music, testimonies, and an informal or relaxed atmosphere.

The three keys to understanding this multicampus ministry are that it was motivated (a) by strength, not weakness, by one of the largest downtown Protestant congregations on the North American continent; (b) not by overcrowding, but rather by a desire to reach and serve people who would not come downtown to church; and (c) by a compelling vision of a new model of ministry for a downtown church in a huge metropolitan area.

The short-term plans call for a temporary meeting place in the huge ballroom of a landmark west side hotel and a continuation of a full-scale downtown ministry by this 153-year-old congregation.

The long-range plans include a continuation of that full-scale downtown ministry and a $35 million construction program on the west campus, including facilities for a K-12 Christian day school.

The impact of this change can be described very simply by looking at Sunday morning. The 1992 schedule called for two traditional worship services, one of which was televised, in that downtown building. The 1993 schedule calls for four worship services every Sunday morning, two at First Church, Downtown, and two at First Church, West. The number of first-time visitors in January 1993 was double the January 1992 total. Worship attendance for the first quarter of 1993 also was up substantially for the first quarter over previous years in which Easter came in April.

The closest to a guaranteed-to-work prescription for that second meeting place includes excellent preaching, a large package of ministries for families with children, a school as the center piece of that package, an extensive teaching ministry with adults, a multifaceted ministry of music, and a series of big events. One of these came in April 1993. The Saturday before Easter featured an Easter Family Festival, including an Easter egg hunt for children. The Easter sunrise service was televised and was followed by breakfast and two later worship services at each site. The plan to include a Christian day school in their design is one reason the Houston venture merits the attention of those intrigued with the multisite option and especially those interested in ministries with families with children. (See chapter 9.)

The Houston experience also illustrates two other facets of this concept. One is that the stronger and the more venturesome the congregation that initiates the design, the more likely it will arouse opposition from other ministers and from denominational officials. If it is proposed by a small, weak congregation that probably will not be able to implement it successfully, it is more likely to evoke support from outsiders. The threat of success can frighten some people.

The other facet is that the greater the resources available to the initiating church, the less likely it will be a significant diversion from the traditional ministry of that initiating congregation. The fewer the available resources, the more likely this plan of action will dominate the congregational agenda. The First United Methodist Church, Houston, experience illustrates the advantages of being able to move from strength.

9.

WHY HAVE A SCHOOL?

Our David doesn't want to go back to school this fall," commented the mother of an eight-year-old boy. She and her husband live in a $250,000 home in an affluent suburb with a first-class public school system.

"Our daughter doesn't want to go back either," commented her friend Tracy, who lives in a middle-income suburban community. It was a beautiful July day, and these two friends were enjoying lunch and conversation in the cafeteria of the company where they both worked.

"Why doesn't David want to go back?" asked Tracy.

"He's convinced he will be shot," was the reply. "When he came home from the final day of school last month, he told me how lucky he was that he hadn't been killed. I thought he was joking, but now I believe he is serious. He's seen so many news stories on TV about children who go to public school being shot, he's convinced that is the norm. To make it worse, on two different occasions last year, older boys in his school were suspended for bringing guns to school. Of course, in both cases every youngster knew about it within a day. Why doesn't your daughter want to go back?"

"Twice last year she was embarrassed because she wet her pants," replied Tracy. "I tell her at breakfast that the most she should drink is a half glass of orange juice and a half glass of milk and not to go near the drinking fountain at school until just before she comes home. If she drinks too much, she has to go to the bathroom, and she is convinced that's not safe at her school. A couple of weeks ago, her closest friend, who has the same problem, told her that she wasn't going back, that her parents had agreed to educate her at home. Our daughter wants us to do that or else let her be taught by the parents of her friend. I would like to do that, but with our mortgage payments, I have to work."

What is the moral of this conversation? Take your pick.

1. **Television prefers bad news over good news.**
2. **Today children's perception of contemporary reality is heavily influenced by television.**
3. **A mother's place is in the home.**
4. **The school day should be shorter.**
5. **The bladders of today's children are too small.**
6. **Parents should teach their children that a high intake of beverages means more trips to the bathroom.**
7. **Teachers should take turns monitoring behavior in the school restrooms.**

An eighth interpretation of this conversation is that fear not only drives the sale of mace, malpractice insurance, hand guns, home security devices, airbags in automobiles, suburban homes, condoms, and nursing home insurance, but fear also is a powerful force in the lives of today's children.

One piece of the oral tradition, according to Mel Brooks and Carl Reiner, is that in 1960 a 2,000-year-old man was brought from the Middle East to New York City. When asked about the means of transportation twenty centuries earlier, the 2,000-year-old man replied, "Mostly fear . . . an animal would growl, you'd go two miles in a minute. Fear would be the main propulsion."[1]

At least a few readers may question this open recognition of fear as a powerful motivational force. Fear, however, is what held Yugoslavia together as one nation for more than four decades. Fear was a powerful force in maintaining the Union of Soviet Socialist Republics. Fear is a favorite motivational tool of lobbyists in Washington, D.C. Fear often determines how a voter will choose between one candidate and another—a vote for one is from fear that the other might be elected. For more than four decades, fear was the number-one force in determining the foreign policy of both the United States and the Union of Soviet Socialist Republics.

While this is far less common today than it was in the nineteenth century, fear often was a favorite motivational tool of preachers. Up until Vatican II, fear was a central organizing principle in the Roman Catholic Church. While it is far from the ideal motivation, fear continues to motivate the lives of many people of all ages in all parts of this planet.[2] The growing enrollment in Protestant schools is only one of many contemporary examples of the power of fear.

Before 1954 one of the two prime motivating factors behind the creation and operation of Christian day schools was the desire to transmit the parents' religious heritage to their children. Back in the post-Civil War era, the fear of the impact on the children of immigrants of the evangelical Protestant culture that permeated the nation's public schools motivated the Roman Catholic bishops to create a huge network of parochial schools. They feared that otherwise the children of Catholic parents would have their religious belief system undermined by the evangelical Protestant religious culture taught in public schools.

That desire to pass their religious culture to the next generation also motivated Lutherans, Seventh Day Adventists, and a few other religious bodies to create their own school systems.

What Do They Fear Today?

The current boom in private Christian schools, and in home schooling, also is fueled in part by fear. Many fear for the physical safety of their children—and that fear is often shared by both parent and child.

A second fear is that "value-free" education will not transmit to the next generation a traditional moral value system. Many parents openly declare that they want help in inculcating a Christian value system in their children. Others prefer that word *traditional.* They want their children to be guided for the rest of their lives by sound values. They identify television, motion pictures, government, the press, and the contemporary American culture as forces that are undermining traditional values. The existence of this fear was demonstrated by the affirmation of traditional "family values" by all three of the major presidential candidates in 1992.

Many children share those fears. "In the public school I went to before I came here, everybody was rowdy; they did what they wanted," explained the daughter of a Chicago public school teacher. "Here, everybody respects everybody," the daughter added to explain why she attends a private Christian school.[3]

Thousands of parents fear that their teenage daughter will become a teenage mother. There is less fear that teenage boys will become fathers because the rate of motherhood among teenage girls is 2.7 times the rate of fatherhood among teenage boys. The explanation is that the average age of teenage mothers has been stable at 18.5 years since at least 1910, while the average age of the fathers of those babies born to teenage mothers has been approximately 21.5 years for twenty years, down from 24 years in 1910.[4] A fair number of parents hope that by sending their daughters to a private school, they will avoid the choice between becoming (a) advocates of divorce or (b) premature grandparents.

More than a few cynics are convinced that the contemporary motivations for enrolling children in private schools are only a polite cover for racism. That may be true with some parents, but three sets of statistics tend to discredit that generalization. The first is that black parents employed in large public school systems are more likely to enroll their children in private schools than are white teachers and administrators. The second is the rapid increase in recent years in the number of black churches that are opening Christian day schools.

The third set of statistics is that the proportion of all students, grades one through twelve, attending private schools in 1985 was 14.2 percent for the Northeast region of the United States, 12.4 percent in North Central states, and 8.2 percent in both the South and the West. The rate of increase from 1979 to 1985 was higher in the Northeast than in the South or West. It also should be noted that Hispanic children from high-income families are more likely to be enrolled in private schools than are either black or white children from high-income families.[5]

A third fear is that the public schools will not instill in children traditional standards of ethical behavior. How do children learn the norms for acceptable behavior? Largely through the modeling of parents, older siblings, teachers, and their peers. Where are children most likely to be exposed to what the parents identify as "good" models of ethical behavior? A growing number are looking to Christian day schools for the answer to that question.

A fourth fear, which many parents cite as their chief motivation for choosing a private school, is that the child will not be challenged to excel in the classroom. Many parents are fearful of the quality and effectiveness of the teaching in many public schools. The "dumbing down" of textbooks, the resistance to anything that could be labeled "elitism," and the drop in the scores on standardized tests of public school graduates have caused an increasing number of parents with upwardly mobile ambitions for their children to choose a private school. (One example of the test score factor is that in 1972 a total of 1,022,820 students took the SAT and 116,630 scored above 600, where the highest possible score is 800. Twenty years later the number taking the SAT increased by one percent, but the number scoring above 600 dropped to 75,243!)

In addition, many parents are disillusioned by the highly visible rewards in public schools for distinction in athletics that are not matched by equally visible rewards for academic performance. What do these rewards for athletic accomplishments in high school communicate to fourth graders about what our society values?

While these four fears are not the only motivating forces, they do help to explain why between 1965 and 1992 the enrollment in non-Catholic private elementary schools in the United States increased from 200,000 to 2.2 million.

Who Will Make It in Tomorrow's World?

Another motivating factor behind the increase in enrollment in Protestant schools is a reflection of the conviction that the adult-oriented contemporary American society with the emphasis on immediate satisfactions over deferred gratification offers a barren and hostile environment for children. What does the future hold for a child born into this environment?

Many parents are convinced that if their child has (1) enjoyed a loving and supportive home environment, (2) mastered basic language skills, (3) learned the rudiments of mathematics, (4) acquired a reasonable level of skill in interpersonal relationships, (5) internalized a traditional moral value system, and (6) practiced and accepted traditional standards of ethical behavior, that youngster can make it in the world. Countless research studies suggest that the first six to ten years of life have a tremendous influence on how that person will function as an adult.

Therefore, these parents look for a school that promises a positive learning environment through grades four or five or six.

After that foundation has been built, the parent assumes that child can make it in the public schools. That helps to explain why the enrollment in non-Catholic religious schools is much higher in grades 1-6 than in grades 7-12. This also is a major factor behind the recent sharp increase in home schooling.

Three Other Factors

If one shifts the focus from asking why more and more Christian parents are either (a) home schooling their children or (b) enrolling them in Christian schools to examining why congregations that do not come from a parochial school heritage are now opening schools, three factors surface immediately. The big one is pressure from parents. The congregation that offers a high-quality weekday nursery-through-kindergarten program naturally will create a lobby from parents of this year's kindergarteners who want that program extended next year to first grade.

A second motivating force is to reach new generations of younger families. This can be a powerful force in the parish that for years has been watching the members grow older in age and fewer in numbers.

The third, and the most highly visible of these three factors, can be seen in the Anglo congregation in the central city that is a victim of white flight. During the 1950–1985 era a common response was to follow the members and relocate the meeting place to a new site in the community to which the members were fleeing.

An alternative is to seek to become a racially integrated or a multicultural congregation. The most effective single strategy for accomplishing that goal in that setting is to open what from day one is a multicultural Christian school with high standards for the students and high expectations of the parents.

This same strategy has been implemented by scores of Afro-Centric, African American, and black congregations in urban

America as they seek to retain the allegiance of their members who are moving to what promises to be "better neighborhoods" while also reaching and serving the newcomer families to the neighborhood in which the meeting place is located and will continue to be located.

The Ideological Alternative

The congregation that decides to open and operate a Christian day school as one component of a larger strategy to minister to families with young children almost always is faced with many challenges and criticisms. One, of course, is the cost of tuition to parents who cannot afford it. That usually is answered either by a sliding fee tuition based on family income or by scholarships or both. A second is charges of elitism. That cannot be denied. Most of these schools are far above average in standards and quality, and they are designed for an elite group of parents— those willing to sacrifice on behalf of their children. President and Mrs. William J. Clinton had to face both of these criticisms when they moved from Little Rock to the White House.

The big criticism, however, is that instead of directing their resources to private Christian schools, the churches should concentrate on improving the public schools. When faced with this ideological argument, one mother asked, "Do you have a proven strategy for reforming the public schools in this city, and how long will it take to implement that strategy?"

The critic answered, "We're working on a strategy that we believe will be effective, and we believe that with the unreserved support of people like you, in ten years we can transform public education in this city."

The mother replied, "I've been hearing that promise ever since I was in first grade, and today the schools here are in worse shape than they were five years ago. More important, in ten years my four-year-old will be in high school, and I'm determined that he will have a good educational foundation before he gets to high school!"

This mother's response illustrates what are four of the most powerful motivations behind the increasing numbers of Protestant Christian schools.

1. **Where do I find hope?**
2. **The urgency of the child's needs cannot wait for reform of the public schools.**
3. **The promises of reform over the past three decades do not offer a foundation for optimism.**
4. **Many parents are more concerned about their children than they are about the potential reform of this nation's political and social institutions.**

Finally, a powerful ideological argument is offered by African American parents, low-income white parents, and other residents of the inner city. "The white parents who want a first-class education for their children flee to the suburbs where state and local taxes pay for high-quality schools. We can't afford the cost of housing in the suburbs. We can't flee. Why should our children be denied a good education just because the public schools can't or won't offer it? If we're willing to make the sacrifices necessary for our children to enroll in a private school here in the inner city, why should the political, religious, and community leaders who live in the suburbs object?"

A parallel argument is offered by Duke University professor William H. Willimon, a United Methodist minister who once opposed Christian day schools. Willimon recently pointed out that Christian schools "are leading the way for a Christian rediscovery of a mission in education . . . and private Christian schools have a potentially very public witness by enacting new ideas that could become the salvation of a tottering public education system."[6]

At least a few Protestant leaders are worried that governmental vouchers that would help finance the cost of sending children to private schools would be a violation of the constitutional guarantee of the separation of church and state. Many constitutional law scholars contend that is not an issue. Carefully drawn legislation could avoid that problem. Church-owned and operated hospitals and nursing homes are being reimbursed for the costs of caring for Medicare and Medicaid patients. Sectarian colleges and universities continue to receive federal grants. Students in religious colleges and theological seminaries continue to be eligible for federally guaranteed loans. Why is it constitutionally acceptable to aid the elderly, the ill, and the college student, but not nine year olds?

In recent years, a growing number of profit-making corporations and business executives in Little Rock, Indianapolis, Atlanta, San Antonio, Milwaukee, and other cities have contributed to the financial support of private Christian schools.

This chapter is not a plea for every congregation to launch a school. It is an attempt, however, to point out that the sectarian motivations that led to the founding of the parochial schools of the late nineteenth century and early twentieth century and the racist attitudes that created the segregationist academies of the 1955–1970 era have been replaced. The generations of parents who enrolled their children in those schools are not the clientele for the Christian day schools of the twenty-first century. Few adults who were in first grade when that famous United States Supreme Court decision on *Brown v. Board of Education* was handed down in 1954 are enrolling children in first grade today. The churches of the twenty-first century are faced with the challenge to reach new generations of parents, and children, who have a new agenda and a new set of concerns.

One model of ministry for accomplishing that is to open a Christian day school on your campus. A parallel model for those interested in planting new congregations to reach new generations is to create a financially self-supporting Christian school as the central component of the teaching ministry of that new mission. A third model for the large suburban congregation with a missionary heart for the central city would be to choose that multisite option described in chapter 7, organize a Christian day school on their inner city campus, and organize a new worshiping community from families who help design and create that school. The easiest-to-implement model for many congregations would be first to extend the present weekday preschool program through kindergarten. The following year first grade would be added. The next year would bring the addition of second grade classes. At the end of six or seven years, this strategy of incremental change would result in a K-6 school.

Which model fits your congregation as you look forward to the twenty-first century?

10.

HOW DO YOU PAY THE BILLS?

What is the most widespread controversial issue that creates divisive debate in congregations today? Abortion? Homosexuality? Placing an American flag in the chancel? A proposal to dismiss the current minister? Revising the Sunday morning schedule? Selling this property and relocating our meeting place to a larger and better site? Deciding whether the confirmation program for older children should run for two years or three? Renovation of the organ? The approach to youth ministries to be utilized with a new generation of teenagers? The numerical decline in the membership?

The correct answer, of course, is none of the above. The most widespread point of internal conflict in congregational life today is over the priorities for allocating scarce financial resources. The second most common point of conflict is over how to raise the money to pay the bills.

Should we encourage designated second-mile giving? Should we tap into the principal of the endowment fund to pay current operating expenses? How much money should we forward to the denomination? Is it acceptable to use investment income for operating expenses or should all income from investments be allocated to missions? What proportion of our total receipts should be allocated to missions and outreach? What proportion should be allocated to compensation of the staff? Should we plan to raise a larger proportion of our total receipts from user fees and sales, and from charging outsiders for use of our building? Or should we seek to become a tithing church? Should we borrow the money to pay for repairs on the roof or should that come out of current income? Should we encourage larger memorial gifts? How can we pay for that needed construction program?

These are but a few of the many divisive questions that surface when church finances are being discussed. What is the best answer to these questions? If we seek to expand our local outreach ministries, how can we pay the bills? That is a complicated set of questions and deserves a book-length answer.[1] For this chapter, however, the response can be divided into three parts.

Financing Capital Expenditures

The first of these three parts of the financial issue concerns expenditures for capital improvements. How can the congregation that wants to explore the multisite option (chapter 8) pay for it? How can the rapidly growing new congregation pay all of the operating expenses and also fund a huge construction program? What can the congregation that has outgrown an inadequate meeting place do when faced with huge capital costs?

Perhaps the best beginning point for examining those and related questions is to look at the contemporary social and economic context. Six changes help to explain the financial squeeze. First, congregations are becoming larger. The parish that averaged 300 to 400 at worship in 1955 was considered a "big" church. The new definition of a "big" congregation is at least 700 at worship. Second, land costs, after allowing for the impact of inflation, are three to ten times what they were in the early 1950s. Third, the cost of renting money has doubled or tripled. The 4 or 5 percent mortgage of 1952 was replaced by a 15 percent interest rate in 1981 and 8 percent in 1993. Fourth, construction costs have gone up faster than the Consumer Price Index.

Fifth, the public's expectations of what represents an acceptable level of quality for schools, motels, grocery stores, restrooms, hospitals, highways, bedrooms, dormitories, garages, and churches has risen substantially during the past half century.

Sixth, the size of an acceptable parcel of land for a congregation's meeting place has climbed from an acre or less in 1950 to ten to two hundred acres today.

One response to that set of trends has been huge capital fund campaigns to pay for that fifteen-acre or larger site and that $3 to $10 million construction program.

Another response has been to seek a nontraditional meeting place. One example of this is Happy Church in suburban Denver. Founded in 1960, this congregation was averaging approximately 1,200 at worship by the late 1980s. As they outgrew their meeting place, their search eventually led to the purchase of an upscale shopping mall built in 1985 on a ten-acre site at a total cost of $34 million. In its best year, it was still two-thirds vacant. By early 1990 the bank that owned it was offering to sell it for $20 million. A few months later, the bank sold it to Happy Church for $7.5 million. This 280,000-square-foot building has 180,000 square feet of usable floor space exclusive of corridors and other open areas and includes 700 covered parking spaces plus additional outdoor parking.

A second example is Calvary Community Church in Phoenix. Founded in 1982 with eleven adults, this congregation met in a school and grew to an average worship attendance of over 700 in eight years. Their search for more room and for a seven-day-a-week facility led to a vacant Revco Drugstore in the Westtown shopping center. They remodeled it to include an auditorium that seats over 900. Their first Sunday morning in the new facility filled that room, and by the third Sunday they were forced to schedule two services.

By early 1993 their attendance was averaging over 1,500. They had leased additional space in the shopping center as it became available and gradually expanded to over 30,000 square feet of leased space.

Instead of investing their money in real estate, by early 1993 they had planted three new missions in Arizona, were helping to support a hundred missionaries, most of them nationals, in other counties, as well as substantial financial support of other local outreach ministries.

(While it is an unrelated subject, one of the unusual facets of what is clearly a contemporary megachurch is the staffing configuration. It is staffed by two pastors, one and one-half paid office positions, nearly three dozen volunteer "flock leaders," and several dozen volunteers who duplicate and mail over 60,000 audio tapes annually. How can they do that? The answer is one that has been emphasized repeatedly in earlier chapters. The four elders carry a very large share of the responsibility for ministry and for shepherding the flock.)

A third response to the problem of capital costs is one of the themes of chapter 7. Instead of closing churches and selling the real estate at a distress price, use the property to reach individuals in that new mission field who have moved into that community. A fourth response is illustrated by the apartment and other campus ministries described in chapter 6. Use what is available. It is not uncommon, for example, for the apartment manager or apartment owner to give that key church one or two apartments rent free. This may be accompanied by a request that the sign or bulletin board publicizing the schedule of that new worshiping community not carry any denominational identification.

For new congregations, the best response to the problem of huge capital costs may be to lease a vacant warehouse or purchase a bankrupt strip shopping center as the first "permanent" meeting place for seven-day-a-week programming. Or it may be possible to purchase a conventional church building at a bargain price from a congregation that is relocating its meeting place. In general, new congregations probably would be wise not to invest in a permanent meeting place until after they are averaging at least 500 or 600 or 700 at worship.

Finally, it may be possible to enter into a joint venture arrangement with another nonprofit organization for construction of multiple use facilities.

How Many Income Streams?

While it does not rank up there in significance with the six paradigm shifts described in chapter 4, a radical change in church finances can be summarized by this descriptive statement: A growing number of congregations have shifted from the offering plate to the cultivation of several income streams in order to pay their bills.

One income stream is the tithes and offerings of members, constituents, and visitors. Some of this is received in the offering plate during the corporate worship of God. A growing proportion is delivered to the church office in the form of cash, checks, stock and bond certificates, and other tangible and intangible assets.

One of the most rapidly growing streams is the income derived from user fees for everything from child care to tuition to trips to meals to fees for special programs, classes, and events. These may include instruction in cardiopulmonary resuscitation or music or Bible study or concerts or income tax preparation or exercise classes or computer skills.

For a small but growing number of congregations in urban America, the fastest growing income stream is from rentals for use of the building. The tenant may be a public school district short of classrooms or a corporation's annual meeting or wedding receptions or Bank Teller Appreciation Night or the offices of a nonprofit agency or a counseling center or a nonprofit child care center. Some of these uses may come very close to violating tax rules on unrelated income, but that is not always a deterrent. One congregation in New York City, for example, underwrites 85 percent of a $460,000 operating budget from rentals.

In 1993 the 32 million Americans age 65 and over controlled over $5 trillion in assets. Dozens of congregations are receiving $3 to $10 million every decade in bequests from longtime members—and occasionally from complete strangers. The typical congregation with $500,000 in receipts annually from member contributions can expect to receive $50,000 to $200,000 or more in bequests each year if a continuing effort is made to encourage members to remember their church in their wills.

Closely related to bequests is another income stream called memorials. Once upon a time memorial gifts usually were in the range of $5 to $25. In today's more affluent society, the range often is $50 to $1,000. If the recently deceased person has left behind a statement of preference for use of these memorial gifts, the total may be substantial. Requests that memorial gifts be used to purchase a van or to renovate a particular room or toward the purchase of a pipe organ or for scholarships are not uncommon. The total amount received in the form of memorial gifts during the course of one year may exceed $10,000.

That major capital funds campaign may yield an amount in two years equal to, double, or triple one year's basic operating budget.

On a smaller scale, the more frequent special appeals for designated causes can yield large sums. One appeal may be for support of foreign missionaries, another to help alleviate world hunger, a third for relief of the victims of a major disaster, a fourth to launch a new off-campus ministry (see chapter 6), a fifth to help heal a wounded bird (see chapter 7), a sixth to add a minister of missions to the staff, and a seventh could be for scholarships for needy children. Ten or fifteen or twenty or forty of these appeals for specific causes can raise an amount equal to one-third to one-half of the basic operating budget.

Investment income is floating to the top as a significant income stream in churches of all sizes. The investments may include money received from (a) bequests, (b) memorials, (c) the receipts from that capital funds campaign between the day the cash is received and the day when the bills must be paid, (d) contributions from members who pay their pledge one or two years in advance, (e) tuition, (f) grants, (g) major gifts contributed in a particular year for tax reasons, but to be spent at a subsequent time, and (h) surplus in the cash flow stream.

A growing number of congregations with extensive community-oriented service ministries, such as a Christian day school, classes in English as a second language, food pantries and soup kitchens, counseling centers, and shelters for the homeless, often are receiving substantial contributions from corporations, local governments, foundations, and individuals who are not members.

In many churches sales produce a net amount equal to 5 to 10 percent of the basic operating budget. The highly visible illustration of this is the bookstore in the church that sells records, tapes, T-shirts, and other merchandise as well as printed resources.

While far from a complete list, these ten income streams illustrate this change in financing ministry at the end of the twentieth century.

Five Models of Congregational Life

A significant number of highly articulate church leaders object to this proliferation of income streams. They contend that if every member were a good and faithful steward of God's gifts, the offering plate would be sufficient. That is an excellent argument and introduces a third perspective for examining congregational finances. This perspective can be illustrated by looking at five models of congregational life.

An all-too-common model is based on the assumption that Christians give to missions and outreach only with great reluctance and therefore the most effective way to raise money is to increase the pressure. The pressure usually includes threats, the use of guilt, defining giving as an obligation, face-to-face confrontations, and publicizing the shortcomings of the delinquents.

A second and better model is the high-expectation congregation that projects high expectations of prospective members. Typically these expectations include (a) regular attendance at the corporate worship of God two or three times every week; (b) active participation in a continuing adult study group; (c) volunteering one's time, money, energy, and talents; (d) tithing and returning that tithe to the Lord via this congregation; and (e) support of that congregation's ministries through prayer.

Typically these congregations report (a) their worship attendance is double or triple their membership and (b) they rarely experience serious financial problems.

A third model is based on the assumption that all financial problems can be eliminated by a powerful continuing and high-quality stewardship education program.

A fourth model is based on two assumptions: (a) the longer a congregation has been in existence, the greater the degree of heterogeneity in the membership and (b) the greater the degree of heterogeneity in the membership, the more useful it is to cultivate at least eight to ten streams of income.

A fifth model operates on the assumption that high-quality ministries designed in response to the needs of today's seekers, searchers, pilgrims, and members will generate the contributions required, not only to sustain that ministry but also to finance an expansion of it to reach more people. When that responsive and high-quality ministry is reinforced by an effective internal communication system, that assumption usually is validated by reality.

Which model is appropriate for your congregation for the third millennium? Which is appropriate for your denomination? Which model is compatible with your values and your goals? Which is the best model for the third millennium?

NOTES

Introduction

1. See Lyle E. Schaller, *The Seven-Day-A-Week Church* (Nashville: Abingdon Press, 1992).

1. Bad News Is Better News Than Good News

1. A plea for a new approach to preparing people for the parish ministry is found in Carolyn Weese, *Standing on the Banks of Tomorrow* (Granada Hills, Calif.: Multi-Staff Ministries, 1993). This writer's contention that excessive and unrealistic expectations have been placed on theological seminaries is in Lyle E. Schaller, *Reflections of a Contrarian* (Nashville: Abingdon Press, 1989), pp. 171-83.

2. For a review of recent trends and patterns in large central-city congregations, see Lyle E. Schaller, ed., *Center City Churches* (Nashville: Abingdon Press, 1993).

3. See Wade Clark Roof, *A Generation of Seekers: The Spiritual Journeys of the Baby Boom Generation* (San Francisco: Harper, 1993).

4. More information on the Parish Nurse Program can be secured by writing National Parish Nurse Resource Center, 1800 Dempster Street, Park Ridge, IL 60068, (708) 696-8773.

5. The rise and decline of comity is reviewed by Lyle E. Schaller, *Planning for Protestantism in Urban America* (Nashville: Abingdon Press, 1965), pp. 96-120.

3. Identify Your Audience

1. Robert Randall, *What People Expect from Church* (Nashville: Abingdon Press, 1993).

2. For a pioneering analysis of the evolution of the role of mainline Protestant denominations, see Craig Dykstra and James Hudnut-Beumler, "The National Organizational Structures of Protestant Denominations: An Invitation to a Conversation," in Milton J. Coalter et al., *The Organizational Revolution: Presbyterians and American Denominationalism* (Louisville: Westminster/John Knox Press, 1992), pp. 307-31.

4. Six Paradigm Shifts

1. Thomas S. Kuhn, *The Structure of Scientific Revolutions* (Chicago: University of Chicago Press, 1962), pp. 23-51.

2. A brief discussion of the emergence of these parachurch organizations can be found in Lyle E. Schaller, *The Seven-Day-A-Week Church* (Nashville: Abingdon Press, 1992), pp. 23-26.

5. The New Partnership

1. Those who want to read more on the challenges facing the larger mainline Protestant denominations may want to begin with Loren Mead, *The Once and Future Church* (Washington, D.C.: The Alban Institute, 1991); Robert Wuthnow, *The Restructuring of American Religion: Society and Faith Since World War II* (Princeton, N.J.: Princeton University Press, 1988); Wade Clark Roof and William McKinney, *American Mainstream Religion: Its Changing Shape and Future* (New Brunswick, N.J.: Rutgers University Press, 1987); Lyle E. Schaller, *The Seven-Day-A-Week Church* (Nashville: Abingdon Press, 1991); James Davison Hunter, *Culture Wars* (New York: Basic Books, 1991); and J. Edward Carothers, *The Paralysis of Mainstream Protestant Leadership* (Nashville: Abingdon Press, 1990). An iconoclastic and provocative account that has won the approval of a few professional church historians is Roger Finke and Rodney Starke, *The Churching of America: Winners and Losers in Our Religious Economy* (New Brunswick, N.J.: Rutgers University Press, 1992). The authors point out that the relative decline of Methodism began in the late nineteenth century. The sixth chapter, "Why Unification Efforts Fail," merits reading by those who are convinced merger is an effective problem-solving tool. An interesting research project on what happened to the confirmands of the 1960s in Presbyterian congregations is Benton Johnson, Dean R. Hoge, and Donald A. Luidens, "Mainline Churches: The Real Reason for Decline," *First Things,* March 1993, pp. 13-18.

2. Milton J. Coalter, John M. Mulder, Louis B. Weeks, eds., *The Presbyterian Presence: The Twentieth Century Experience,* 7 vols. (Louisville: Westminster/John Knox Press, 1992).

3. This brief review of the experiences of the Gambrell Street Baptist Church has drawn heavily from an unpublished paper written by J. Timothy Ahlen, dated November 1, 1991. I also am indebted to him for constructive reading of an earlier draft of this chapter.

4. Much of this discussion, including these six criteria, is drawn from the manual by JV Thomas, *The Key Church Strategy* (Atlanta: Home Mission Board, n.d.)

6. Off-Campus Ministries

1. An excellent resource that spells out the how-to-do-it process in greater detail is David T. Bunch, Harvey J. Kneisel, and Barbara J. Oden, *Multihousing Congregations* (Atlanta: Smith Publishing, 1991).
2. A useful resource for nursing home ministries is Agnes P. Schaller and Analee L. Kinney, *Never Too Old to Have Fun: Seasonal Parties for Seasoned Citizens* (Nashville: Abingdon Press, 1993).
3. For the importance of physical place in people's lives, see Lyle E. Schaller, *Effective Church Planning* (Nashville: Abingdon Press, 1979), pp. 65-92. See also Winifred Gallagher, *The Power of Place* (New York: Poseidon Press, 1993).

7. What About the Wounded Birds?

1. For a completely different perspective on wounded birds and disabled congregations, see John David Webb, *How to Change the Image of Your Church* (Nashville: Abingdon Press, 1993).
2. For one perspective on congregational mergers, see Lyle E. Schaller, *Reflections of a Contrarian* (Nashville: Abingdon Press, 1989), pp. 136-49.

8. The Multisite Option

1. An excellent discussion of congregational experiences with the multisite option is W. Jere Allen, "Become One Church in Two Locations," in Phillip E. Rodgerson, ed., *Choices for Churches in Changing Communities* (Atlanta: Home Mission Board, SBC, n.d.), pp. 59-62.
2. For suggestions on implementing the relocation alternative, see Lyle E. Schaller, *Choices for Churches* (Nashville: Abingdon Press, 1990), pp. 97-121.
3. A more detailed account of this struggle can be found in Barry L. Johnson, "By Faith . . . Together!" in Robert L. Burt, ed., *Good News in Growing Churches* (New York: Pilgrim Press, 1990), pp. 65-87.
4. See Lyle E. Schaller, *Strategies for Change* (Nashville: Abingdon Press, 1993), pp. 67-78.
5. For a more detailed discussion of fair expectations of committees, see Lyle E. Schaller, *Getting Things Done* (Nashville: Abingdon Press, 1986), chaps. 6 and 7.

9. Why Have a School?

1. Mel Brooks and Carl Reiner, *The 2,000 Year Old Man* (New York: Warner Books, 1981), p. 7.

2. A relevant account of how fear can be a powerful motivating force in national politics is Robert Griffith, *The Politics of Fear: Joseph R. McCarthy and the Senate* (New York: The Hayden Book Company, Inc., 1970).

3. A teenager's perspective on this issue is reflected in Francis A. J. Ianni, *The Search for Structure: A Report on American Youth Today* (New York: The Free Press, 1989).

4. Mike Males, "Schools, Society and 'Teen' Pregnancy," *Phi Delta Kappan* (March 1993): 566-68.

5. *Private Schools in the United States: A Statistical Profile with Comparisons to Public Schools* (Washington, D.C.: U. S. Government Printing Office, February, 1991).

6. William H. Willimon, "I Was Wrong About Christian Schools," *Christianity Today,* February 8, 1993, pp. 30-32. For an excellent analysis of why recent efforts to reform America's public schools have failed, see Thomas Toch, *In the Name of Excellence* (New York: Oxford University Press, 1991).

10. How Do You Pay the Bills?

1. For a more extensive discussion of the revenue side of the ledger, see Lyle E. Schaller, *44 Ways to Expand the Financial Base of Your Congregation* (Nashville: Abingdon Press, 1989).

4408